D0803325

Zell, Fran, 1947–
A multicultural portrait
of the American
c1996 WITHDRAWN
33305006913804
MH   02/10/97

PERSPECTIVES

A Multicultural Portrait of

The American Revolution

By Fran Zell

BENCHMARK BOOKS

MARSHALL CAVENDISH
NEW YORK

SANTA CLARA COUNTY LIBRARY

3 3305 00691 3804

Cover: A detail from an artist's view of the Battle of Lexington, where the American Revolution officially began in April 1775. More than seventy minutemen faced down the British in Lexington and in the neighboring Massachusetts village of Concord. At least nine of these able voluneers were of African descent.

Benchmark Books
Marshall Cavendish Corporation
99 White Plains Road
Tarrytown, New York 10591-9001, U.S.A.

© Marshall Cavendish Corporation, 1996

Edited, designed, and produced by Water Buffalo Books, Milwaukee

All rights reserved. No part of this book may be reproduced or utilized in any form or by any means electronic or mechanical, including photocopying or recording, or by any information storage and retrieval system, without permission from the copyright holders.

Editorial consultant: Richard Taylor, History Department (Adjunct), the University of Wisconsin-Parkside

Picture Credits: © Archive Photos: 8, 28; © The Bettmann Archive: Cover, 6, 10, 11, 12, 14, 15, 17, 20-21, 23, 25, 27, 29, 34-35, 36, 40, 42, 44, 46, 48, 50, 52, 53, 54, 55 (both), 56, 61, 62-63, 69, 71, 72, 73, 75; © Culver Pictures: 18, 19, 51, 59, 60, 64, 65; © H. Armstrong Roberts: 31, 41

Library of Congress Cataloging-in-Publication Data

Zell, Fran.
    A multicultural portrait of the American Revolution / by Fran Zell.
       p.   cm. -- (Perspectives (Marshall Cavendish Corporation))
    Includes bibliographical references and index.
    Summary: Describes the history of the American Revolution, focusing on the lives of Afro-Americans, Native Americans, and women.
    ISBN 0-7614-0051-6 (lib. bdg.)
    1. United States--History--Revolution, 1775-1783--Social aspects--Juvenile literature. 2. Minorities--United States--History--18th century--Juvenile literature. 3. Pluralism (Social sciences)--United States--History--18th century--Juvenile literature [1. United States--History--Revolution, 1775-1783. 2. Afro-Americans--History. 3. Indians of North America--History. 4. Women--History. 5. Minorities--History.] I. Title. II. Series.
    E209.Z45   1995
    973.3'1--dc20
                                                95-11032
                                                 CIP
                                                   AC

To PS – MS

Printed in Malaysia
Bound in the U.S.A.

CONTENTS

About *Perspectives*

Perspectives is a series of multicultural portraits of events and topics in U.S. history. Each volume examines these events and topics not only from the perspective of the white European-Americans who make up the majority of the U.S. population, but also from that of the nation's many people of color and other ethnic minorities, such as African-Americans, Asian-Americans, Hispanic-Americans, and American Indians. These people, along with women, have been given little attention in traditional accounts of U.S. history. And yet their impact on historical events has been great.

The terms *American Indian, Native American, Hispanic-American, Latino, Anglo-American, Black, African-American,* and *Asian-American,* like *European-American* and *white,* are used by the authors in this series to identify people of various national origins. Labeling people is a serious business, and what we call a group depends on many things. For example, a few decades ago it was considered acceptable to use the words *colored* or *Negro* to label Americans of African origin. Today, these words are outdated and often a sign of ignorance or outright prejudice. Some even consider *Black* less acceptable than *African-American* because it focuses on a person's skin color rather than national origins. And yet *Black* has many practical uses, especially to describe people whose origins are not only African but Caribbean or Latin American as well.

If we must label people, it is better to be as specific as possible. That is a goal of *Perspectives* — to be as precise and fair as possible in the labeling of people by race, ethnicity, national origin, or other factors, such as gender, sexual orientation, or disability. When necessary and possible, Americans of Mexican origin will be called *Mexican-Americans.* Americans of Irish origin will be called *Irish-Americans,* and so on. The same goes for American Indians: When possible, specific Indians are identified by their tribal names, such as *Winnebago* or *Mohawk.* But in a discussion of various Indian groups, tribal origins may not always be entirely clear, and so it may be more practical to use *American Indian,* a term that has widespread use among Indians and non-Indians alike.

Even within a group, individuals may disagree over the labels they prefer for their group: *Black* or *African-American? American Indian* or *Native American? Hispanic* or *Latino? White, Anglo,* or *European-American?* Different situations often call for different labels. The labels used in *Perspectives* represent an attempt to be fair, accurate, and perhaps most importantly, to be mindful of what people choose to call *themselves.*

A Note About *The American Revolution*

In April 1775, "the shot heard 'round the world" at Lexington and Concord, Massachusetts, launched the thirteen American colonies into a fierce battle with England that would result in the birth of the United States as a democratic nation dedicated to the idea of freedom and equality for all people. The American Revolution lasted eight years, took many lives, destroyed much property, and exacted great hardship on everyone it touched.

It was also a time of great awakening for the early residents of this country. In joining together as an independent nation, they had to face the fact that they were a diverse people who did not all react to the war in the same way. Many people favored the break with England, but many supported the British Crown. Much of the population felt excluded by this important fight for freedom and made its feelings known, sometimes — in keeping with the mood of the times — quite violently. Many growing pains lay ahead for the young nation at war, including problems around issues of equality and civil liberties that are still unsolved today.

The white European men who wrote the Declaration of Independence spoke of "life, liberty, and the pursuit of happiness" at a time when Africans were enslaved and sold on the auction block like cattle, when American Indians were losing their ancestral lands to white settlers, and when Blacks (free or slave), Indians, women, and poor, propertyless white men were considered unqualified to vote or hold public office.

Yet many members of these groups knew about the Declaration of Independence and celebrated its words because it spoke to their dreams and hopes, too. This book will take a close look at what life was like during the Revolution for Africans, Native Americans, poor European settlers, and women, as well for the upper-class European men who generally receive most of the attention in history books about the war for independence. You will learn about the great contributions these diverse people made to the birth of the United States. You will also learn about different attitudes members of these groups held toward the war and how all these feelings were shaped by their desire for a better life.

In the North, thousands of Blacks, free and slave alike, fought for the Revolutionary cause. Thousands more, mostly in the South, supported England because it offered them what they believed was their only chance for freedom. Most Indians also supported the British because they distrusted the European settlers and their constant hunger for land. Many European settlers sided with England for political, religious, and personal reasons. Some people, particularly the Quakers, who are against the idea of war, tried not to take any side at all.

By looking at the American Revolution from a multicultural perspective, you will see that war has many faces and that sometimes it is important to look at each of these faces as if it were our own. The American Revolution left us a great legacy in the form of a democratic government with a Constitution that guarantees basic freedoms to everyone. But if the diverse people that populate this nation today are to deal with their many problems in a just, peaceful way, they must learn to understand what it is like to walk in each other's shoes.

Crispus Attucks lies mortally wounded at the Boston Massacre, March 5, 1770. Attucks, the son of an African father and American Indian mother, led the first confrontation between colonists and British soldiers that resulted in death. A runaway slave, Attucks was the first of five men to die in the fray.

CHAPTER ONE

Trouble Brews:
Strained Relations with England

The year most often given as the beginning of the American Revolution is 1775. That was the year that colonial minutemen and British soldiers clashed at Concord and Lexington, Massachusetts. But five years earlier, 1770, was when the first man died in what would be the American Revolution. This man was a former slave named Crispus Attucks.

Attucks was the son of an African father and an American Indian mother from the Natick tribe. Even as a slave in Framingham, Massachusetts, he tried to be independent, earning his own money as a horse and cattle trader. Unable to buy his freedom, he ran away.

His owner advertised for his return, but Attucks was not heard from in Massachusetts for twenty years. He may have found work on whaling ships. But on the icy night of March 5, 1770, Attucks resurfaced in Boston. Perhaps because he saw a connection between slavery and the inferior position of the colonists, Attucks led a band of citizens down a hilly street toward well-armed British soldiers.

There had been tension between soldiers and workingmen in Boston because soldiers were allowed to take jobs as laborers in a time of high unemployment. This meant fewer jobs and lower wages for colonial men. On the night of March 5, a soldier hit a boy on the head with his gun. Church bells rang an alarm, and an angry crowd gathered.

"Damn them, they dare not fire, we are not afraid of them," Attucks shouted, waving a long stick at the redcoats as they faced each other near the Customs House. People heckled the soldiers, throwing snowballs, stones, and sticks. With a yell, Attucks clubbed a soldier. A hail of snowballs, chunks of ice, and rocks followed. The English replied with gunfire. Attucks fell first, hit twice in the chest. Four other civilians died and six more were wounded in what became known as the Boston Massacre.

Crispus Attucks: A man as property

"Ran away from his Master William Brown of Framingham . . . a Molatto Fellow, about 27 years of age, named Crispas, six feet two Inches high, short curl'd Hair, his Knees nearer together than common; had on a light colour'd Bearskin Coat . . . new Buckskin Breeches, blue Yarn Stockings, and a check'd woollen Shirt.

"Whoever shall take up said Run-away, and convey him to his aforementioned Master, shall have ten Pounds old Tenor Reward, and all necessary Charges paid. And all Masters . . . are hereby caution'd against concealing or carrying off said Servant on Penalty of the Law."

— Advertisment placed in the *Boston Gazette*, October 2, 1750, by William Brown of Framingham, Massachusetts, regarding his runaway slave, Crispus Attucks. Attucks remained free for twenty years and died making a stand for freedom at the Boston Massacre.

A Hero's Funeral

Thousands of people marched in a funeral procession for the five victims. More than a hundred years later, in 1888, a monument was erected on Boston Common to honor Attucks.

The British soldiers who took part in the Boston Massacre were tried for murder and acquitted. One of their defense lawyers was John Adams, the same John Adams who would sign the Declaration of Independence. In 1770, Adams condemned the victims as rabble-rousers. But a few years later, he spoke differently, realizing that Attucks and the others had struck a blow for freedom against English rule, changing the course of history.

Many events took place in the thirteen colonies that resulted in violence between the colonists and England. To understand the situation better, we need to return to 1763, when tensions that would lead to the Revolutionary War began to build.

English Power Leads to Conflict

England was powerful in 1763. It had just defeated France in the Seven Years' War, also known as the French and Indian War. In addition to controlling the colonies, England controlled all the land in North America from the Appalachian Mountains on the east to the Mississippi River on the west, including much of Canada. Thousands of soldiers were sent to North America to defend this newly acquired land and keep the peace. England ordered the colonists to pay for this protection.

The war with France cost England more than any other war it had ever fought. When it ended, England's national debt had nearly doubled. Much of the fighting had been done by British soldiers, with British citizens paying most of the taxes to support the military.

The war changed the way England looked at the American colonies. Until 1763, England viewed the New World as a big investor might view a business partner. The colonies produced raw materials, which England needed, and in return bought goods England produced. England governed loosely until 1763, allowing colonial leaders to make their own decisions. Each colony had a governor appointed by the king and an assembly elected by property-owning colonial men. The governors often were lax about enforcing English laws that affected business practices, and the colonial legislators passed laws to protect the rights of the white men they represented.

Over the years, the New England colonies produced goods England did not need. They sold such goods — fish, timber, and beans — to the French and Spanish West Indies in exchange for sugar and molasses. They also traded directly with France, the Netherlands, Germany, and Sweden, mostly for tea. Such transactions were illegal; the colonies were not supposed to trade with countries other than England. But until 1763, England did not stop them.

After 1763, England wanted more control. It felt the colonists were indebted because English soldiers and money had protected them in the French and Indian War, even though the war also helped England expand its empire. The mother country saw the colonists with the same sort of superiority with which white settlers viewed American Indians and Africans. In general, the colonists and the British no longer had a common enemy, so they turned on each other.

New Laws Anger Colonists

The British Parliament passed many new laws to raise money for support of British troops in the New World, including these:

• **The Revenue Act or the Sugar Act of 1764,** which placed duties on products imported from the French West Indies, especially molasses and sugar. The law was designed to force merchants to trade only with England.

• **The Currency Act of 1764,** which forbade colonists from printing money or starting their own banks. This law hurt an already weak colonial economy.

• **The Quartering Act of 1765,** which required that colonists pay to build barracks for British soldiers and supply their provisions.

• **The Stamp Act of 1765,** which ordered the purchase and use of stamps on newspapers, pamphlets, and legal documents, as well as on playing cards and dice. It also taxed the price of an indentured servant and the contract between a craftsman and an apprentice.

To enforce these laws, England sent over customs and revenue collectors, stamp officials, and enforcement agents. The laws angered the colonists, and so did the new officials, who often enforced those laws by seizing merchants' goods as payment.

Colonists argue with British officials about the Stamp Act of 1765. The law placed taxes on newspapers, legal contracts, and other printed materials. Anger over the law led to riots in cities throughout the colonies, and it was soon repealed.

Taxation without Representation

Many American colonists were outraged by the Stamp Act. People of all social classes, especially in the cities, felt it was an illegal tax because it was imposed by England instead of by their own elected officials. They called it taxation without representation — they were paying to support a government, but they had no voice in how the government was run. The British, colonists believed, were taking away their freedoms. Wealthy merchants, lawyers, printers, tavern keepers, and some planters were most directly affected by the Stamp Act.

The law hurt middle-class people, too, in particular independent trades- and craftspeople, such as silversmiths, blacksmiths, woodworkers, shoemakers, bakers, and tailors who struggled to own their own businesses. Taxes forced prices up, making it more expensive to compete with English products. Laborers and other working people were not directly affected by the Stamp Act, but like Crispus Attucks, they were angry about British soldiers who worked for low wages, driving down everyone's pay.

There was violence in the colonies as a result of the Stamp Act. People rioted, burning the stamps, and merchants in port cities refused to order British goods. Only a year after being allied against the French and the Indians, England and the colonies were in an ugly confrontation. England repealed the law in 1766.

After the repeal of the Stamp Act, the question of how to govern the colonies became as important to England as the question of how to raise money. In 1767, the British Parliament passed the Townshend Acts, placing import duties on British goods such as paper, paint, glass, and tea. Parliament established a customs agency in Boston to collect the duties. Again there were protests. Newspapers railed against British tyranny, labeling the duties a tax in disguise. People boycotted British goods, growing angrier at the British soldiers in their towns. In 1770, England again bowed to the pressure and removed all duties except on tea.

Colonial wholesalers smuggled tea from the Netherlands to avoid the British duty, and England lost tax money. In 1773, Parliament passed the Tea Act. This enabled England to sell tea directly to colonial retailers and made British tea cheaper than Dutch tea, even with the tariff, because it eliminated the middleman. English lawmakers assumed everyone would buy British tea and stop complaining. They further assumed the wholesalers would stop smuggling Dutch tea. Public opinion, however, remained against England. On December 16, 1773, at least two thousand people attended a meeting in Boston to object to the Tea Act.

The Boston Tea Party

After the meeting, two hundred colonists dressed as Mohawk Indians boarded British ships in the Boston harbor and threw 342 chests of tea into the sea. The event would be remembered as the Boston Tea Party. British leaders were furious — the colonists had destroyed tea worth thousands of dollars. Britain wanted to set an example by punishing Tea Party participants. They quickly passed several laws that came to be called the Intolerable Acts. One closed the port until Bostonians paid for the tea. Another restricted the Massachusetts legislature and increased the powers of the English-appointed governor.

Two hundred colonists dressed as Mohawk Indians dump tea from British ships into Boston Harbor in protest over England's 1773 Tea Act. The Boston Tea Party, as it would become known, raised tensions between England and the colonies to new levels.

Mother of the Boston Tea Party

On the night of December 16, 1773, Sarah and John Fulton invited friends over for Sarah's codfish chowder. They would afterward attend a crowded town meeting where the royal governor told them they would have to pay the tax on tea recently arrived on ships in Boston Harbor. After the meeting, many men gathered in the carpenter shop attached to the Fulton house; it was a meeting place for the Sons of Liberty.

Sarah and her sister were in the center of the crowd, helping men redden their skin and wrap themselves in blankets — Mohawk Indian disguises they would wear when they dumped the tea into the sea. Later that evening, Mrs. Fulton heated water in her kitchen so the men could remove their disguises. For her part in this historical event, Sarah Fulton earned the title Mother of the Boston Tea Party. (The Mohawk did not really have red skin, but like other northeastern Indian people, they covered their skin with a mixture of bear grease and red pigment to protect it from insects in the summer and to keep it from chapping in the winter.)

Members of a patriotic group known as the "Sons of Liberty" brawl with British soldiers. Some intentionally provoke the soldiers, street-fighter style. Fights like this one were common after England began passing objectionable tax laws.

Colonial-English Violence Grows

The Boston Massacre in March 1770 was just one clash that led to the American Revolution. Rioting took place in several cities. As living conditions grew worse, it took very little to turn a crowd of unemployed boys and men against wealthy British officials. Two months before the Boston Massacre, a larger run-in took place in New York between British troops and members of a patriotic group called the Sons of Liberty. No one was killed, but many were badly hurt on both sides.

The Sons of Liberty formed in 1765 after England passed the Stamp Act. Members were a cross-section of white colonists, from wealthy lawyers and merchants to tradesmen, shopkeepers, and workingmen. Wealthy leaders recruited young street fighters and gang members.

The Sons of Liberty organized riots in Boston that spread throughout the colonies after the Stamp Act. Mobs threatened stamp distributors and other royal officials, in a few cases burning and plundering their homes. The Sons of Liberty were associated with violence from the outset, making some wealthier members reluctant to associate with the group. They did, however, bring very different people together for a common cause.

They also showed the value of the kind of unified protests that forced England to repeal the Stamp Act less than a year after it went into effect.

Colonial Women Help the Cause

Colonial women could not vote, but they played an important role in the turbulent years leading to the Revolution. In New England, they attended town meetings where colonists pledged resistance to the new British laws. Abigail Adams held her own strongly felt opinions and beliefs, and she encouraged her husband John as he wrote resolutions that were adopted at the meeting held in their Massachusetts town in response to the Stamp Act.

Throughout the colonies, women formed groups called Daughters of Liberty. They played a major role in boycotting British goods to protest the Intolerable Acts. In Pepperell, Massachusetts, women burned tea in front of the meeting house to protest the Tea Act of 1773. Led by Penelope Barker, women of Edenton, North Carolina, resolved that they would neither drink English tea nor wear English clothes until the tea tax was removed.

For years, Nancy Warren of Plymouth, Massachusetts, wrote letters discussing colonial problems; her brother, James Otis, a Massachusetts assemblyman, circulated these letters widely among other colonial leaders. Warren also corresponded about political issues with her friend, Abigail Adams. Warren's letters helped develop Committees of Correspondence, which kept colonial leaders informed of news in the feud with England.

The First Continental Congress

Eventually, however, letters were not enough. Throughout the colonies, upper- and middle-class men formed committees warning each other that England might curtail political rights by destroying colonial legislatures, as it had done in Massachusetts following the Boston Tea Party. The men decided to meet in September 1774 to discuss ways of resisting the Intolerable Acts and protecting their freedom. Fifty-six men representing the thirteen colonies gathered in Philadelphia. They were all wealthy white men and colonial leaders. Many would become heroes, immortalized for more than two centuries of American history: John Adams and his cousin Samuel from Massachusetts; John Jay from New York; Patrick Henry, Thomas Jefferson, and George Washington, all from Virginia. Their meeting would be known as the Continental Congress.

The delegates agreed that their rights were being violated by England, yet they brought different interests and views to Philadelphia. Some, especially southern delegates, were conservative. They considered themselves Englishmen first and wanted to keep the peace. They disliked mob action, fearing the poor eventually might turn on wealthy people like themselves. Some northern delegates, especially those from troubled Boston and Philadelphia, were far more radical. They were willing to push England to the brink of war.

What the delegates agreed to was this: They would break off all trade with England, including slave trade. They would not act alone, as individual colonies, as they had in the past. Instead, they would act as a group, which they called the Continental Association. And they would set up committees to enforce boycotting British goods until England stopped unreasonable taxation. England, of course, would never agree to such terms — it needed the income. Battle lines were drawn by a number of men who had fought for the British only eleven years earlier.

Continental Congress delegates did not address the rights of everyone. Many delegates were slave owners, and others backed western expansion that was pushing American Indians from their land. The slave trade was a major business for England; by discontinuing it, the delegates were hoping to pressure England into repealing objectionable taxes. Abolitionists, however, were hopeful that slavery itself might soon be abolished. Unfortunately, this was not to be.

Slaves Cry for Liberty

There was a huge contradiction in the cries for freedom and liberty among white colonists during the 1760s: People spoke of inalienable natural rights and equality while nearly 20 percent of the population was enslaved. Blacks noticed this discrepancy and acted on it. From 1765 to 1785, there was more unrest among slaves throughout the colonies than in any previous period.

In Boston, the spirit of Crispus Attucks inspired a large group of slaves to ask the government of Massachusetts to end slavery. These slaves had four leaders — Peter Bestes, Sambo Freeman, Chester Joie, and Felix Holbrook. They told the governor and the legislature how they felt in 1773 and 1774.

"We expect great things from men who have made such a noble stand against the designs of their fellowmen to enslave them," read a letter to the Massachusetts House of Representatives. Slaves asked the lawmakers to allow them one day each week to work for themselves so they could earn enough money to buy their freedom. They wanted to leave America and start their own settlement in Africa. "We have no Property! We have no Wives! No Children. We have no City! No Country!" the slaves told Governor Hutchinson in another letter.

Slaves arrive in Jamestown, Virginia, on a Dutch ship. The institution of slavery contradicted colonists' cries for freedom and liberty for all, and many slaves spoke out for their freedom during the time of the Revolution.

Antislavery Sentiment Grows

Antislavery feelings also were developing among some whites in Massachusetts at the time. But the government took no action in response to slaves' pleas for freedom. Ten years would pass before Massachusetts outlawed slavery.

Most northern slaves by the mid-1760s were American born. They spoke English and tended to live in cities, so they understood the conflict between colonists and the crown. Slaves in the South were more isolated and so were less aware of the reasons behind the struggle with England. But they knew about the dispute and were no less concerned about freedom.

"Liberty! Liberty!" a group of male slaves chanted in Charleston, South Carolina, in 1766, echoing cries heard from white crowds protesting the Stamp Act. Rumors of a slave revolt quickly spread. A few years earlier, some South Carolina slave owners had been killed with poison by desperate slaves; European colonists became frightened. The South Carolina legislature passed a tax designed to reduce the number of slaves brought in from Africa. In 1765, more than seven thousand slaves had been imported. The following year, after the tax, only 101 slaves arrived.

An auctioneer asks for bids at a slave sale. Neither the auctioneer nor the many people gathered around to buy or watch questioned the morality of selling humans as cargo.

The slaves' communication system

Southern slaves had a well-developed system for acquiring and passing on information about their masters' lives and politics. Household slaves overheard conversations when they were serving food or otherwise attending their owners. They carried the news back to the slave quarters, and from there, it would travel to other plantations and even other colonies via a network of slaves who were sent elsewhere to live or work. In this way, enslaved people followed Revolutionary War news and events leading up to it. At the Continental Congress in 1774, two Georgia delegates told John Adams that the slave network could carry news "several hundreds of miles in a week or a fortnight."

Some colonists saw slavery as a curse during the pre-Revolutionary decade, and their awareness gave rise to the abolitionist movement. Most abolitionists lived in the North; many were ministers, and some were Revolutionary leaders. In 1764, James Otis, then a member of the Massachusetts House of Representatives, published a widely read book that argued for the rights of whites and Blacks alike. He wrote, "The Colonists are by the law of nature free born, as indeed all men are, white or black. . . . Does it follow that 'tis right to enslave a man because he is black?"

John Woolman, a Quaker minister, warned that European colonists were imprisoning their souls when they looked down on African slaves. Thomas Jefferson lamented the "unremitting despotism" of slave owners, yet he continued to own slaves. In 1774, Abigail Adams wrote to her husband, John, "I wish most sincerely there was not a slave in the province, it always appeared a most iniquitous scheme to me to fight ourselves for what we are daily robbing and plundering from those who have as good a right to freedom as we have."

The abolitionists made headway in the North. Before the Declaration of Independence in 1776, many northern colonies did away with the slave trade or taxed it out of existence. They did not, however, outlaw slavery. The issue was much less important to the average resident than was the coming conflict with Britain.

Slavery Survives in the South

The abolitionist movement was weak in the South, where nine of ten slaves lived and where it would have made the biggest difference. Swayed by prejudice, many white colonists convinced themselves there was no connection between their struggle for freedom and the plight of the slave. The southern economy was based on slavery, and slaves brought large planters wealth, power, and prestige. Instead of worrying about the slave's welfare, they fretted over their investment.

This callous attitude led to increased unrest among southern slaves. In December 1774, a group of ten male and female slaves in Georgia killed their overseer, his wife, and a boy and seriously wounded two other white colonists. The slaves were captured and killed.

The British knew that some southern slave owners feared their slaves would turn against them if they were free. They took advantage of this fear, telling slave owners in some southern colonies that if they did not accept the new English policies, England would free their slaves. At the same time, England encouraged slaves to rebel, promising them freedom. Ultimately, British interference convinced many colonists in the South to go to war with England. In their quest for freedom and dignity, however, Blacks in the South were eager to support England.

Crowding the Indians

When the French and Indian War ended in 1763, England gained control over the profitable French fur trade with Native Americans. However, the British failed to give the Indians a fair exchange for the furs, treating them with contempt. Most Indians had supported France in the war, and the British wanted

A Native woman of the Northeast sits in her tribe's menstruation lodge. Indians considered this phase of the reproductive cycle a highly spiritual time, one of great personal power for women.

to punish them. Indians preferred the French because their trappers did not overrun Native land. The French also tended to recognize and respect cultural differences among tribes.

England's King George III decided it would be best for whites to live separately from Indians until an orderly way could be found to settle the newly acquired territory. He issued the Proclamation of 1763, which declared that American Indians had the right to all land west of the Appalachian Mountains. White settlers were to remain east of the Appalachian divide.

England never really enforced this law, which settlers ignored. Natives had been led to expect protection from settlers by the British. But they were continually disappointed as treaties were made, then broken or ignored, and settlers continued to push westward.

Violence on the Frontier

Violence against Indians was common. For example, seventy-five Pennsylvania frontiersmen calling themselves the Paxton Boys massacred all twenty members of a Susquehannock village in 1763. They then broke into a jail and killed fourteen Susquehannock who had hidden there. Later, the Paxton Boys marched toward Philadelphia, vowing to kill Indians there. The normally peaceful Quakers prepared to fight, and Benjamin Franklin headed a delegation that talked the Paxtons out of their killing spree.

The British often took advantage of tribal rivalries by stirring up wars among various groups and encouraging them to cheat one another. In 1768, the Iroquois sold land they did not occupy to British and colonial officials in an agreement called the Treaty of Fort Stanwix. The treaty angered the Shawnee, whose lands were threatened by an influx of settlers into southwestern Pennsylvania and central Kentucky.

The value of American Indian education

In 1774, chiefs of the Six Nations (a confederacy of Iroquois and Tuscarora tribes) protested to Benjamin Franklin that the schools white colonists wanted native sons to attend turned them away from their heritage. Here is what one chief said: "But you, who are wise, must know that different nations have different conceptions of things; and you will therefore not take it amiss, if our ideas of this kind of education happen not to be the same with yours. We have had some experience of it — several of our young people were formerly brought up at the colleges of northern provinces; they were instructed in all your sciences, but when they came back to us, they were bad runners, ignorant of every means of living in the woods, unable to bear either cold or hunger, knew neither how to build a cabin, take a deer, or kill an enemy, spoke our language imperfectly, were therefore neither fit for hunters, warriors, nor counsellors; they were totally good for nothing. We are however not the less obliged by your kind offer, though we decline accepting it, and, to show our grateful sense of it, if the gentlemen of Virginia will send us a dozen of their sons, we will take great care of their education, instruct them in all we know, and make men of them."

An Indian family gathers at home after a productive day of fishing. Most Indians lived in settled communities where hunting and fishing supplemented their farming activities.

The Shawnee asked the Creek and Cherokee to unite with them in a war against the British and white settlers. However, the Creek and Cherokee were longtime rivals, and the British persuaded them not to join with the Shawnee; both tribes were soon tricked out of land themselves. In 1773, the Creek were forced to give more than two million acres to Georgia for debts the Indians owed British traders. The Cherokee lost land in a deal with Virginia after surveyors made a mistake that was never corrected, even though colonial officials knew of the error.

Lord Dunmore's War

The Shawnee eventually fought against whites in a conflict known as Lord Dunmore's War of 1774. They had been promised that white settlers would not enter their Kentucky hunting areas; settlers arrived anyway, encouraged by Lord Dunmore, Virginia's governor. Dunmore had awarded the land to veterans of the French and Indian war. After bloody clashes between Shawnees and settlers, Dunmore called up the Virginia militia. The Shawnee's Chief Cornstalk tried to avoid war, but with the militia on the scene, he led his tribe against the Virginians. The Shawnee appealed to the Iroquois League for help but received help only from the Seneca, whose chief had lost kin in an earlier skirmish. The Shawnee soon retreated north of the Ohio River, giving up their claim to the disputed land.

Indian versus Indian

The inability of Indians to unite eventually hurt all Natives. Only occasionally did leaders persuade individual groups to forget their differences and act together. Then, too, the British and other Europeans were skilled at pitting tribes and nations against each other. Before the white man's arrival, wars had occurred between tribes, but for different reasons — war was one way for men to prove their courage. Battles were brief and far less destructive than those with the settlers.

With the arrival of Europeans, the stakes changed. Natives enjoyed the goods they received by trading furs in the North and, in the South, escaped slaves whom they captured and returned. These goods included tools, guns, bullets, clothing materials, and other items that made life easier and changed the way they farmed, hunted, and protected themselves. They also received rum, which made them sick or violent, as it did whites. Various Indians competed with each other for these goods and for territory in which to hunt animals for furs. As a result, Native tribes fought bitterly, sometimes wiping each other out.

When the Revolution began, most Natives turned their loyalties toward England. Many remained neutral as long as possible, pleased that there was a war between their enemies. Yet they knew that war involving any white men rarely worked to their advantage.

Two Indian leaders end a long-standing dispute with violence. Rivalry was not uncommon between tribes, a fact that European settlers often took advantage of by providing Natives with weapons and new reasons to fight each other.

The great Ottawa chief, Pontiac, meets in council with leaders from various Indian nations. In 1763, Pontiac urged his people to fight against British injustices. The Indians were defeated in the resulting war, known as Pontiac's Uprising.

CHAPTER TWO

On the Eve of Revolution: A Changing People

The American Revolution began with "the shot heard 'round the world." No one is sure who fired that first round in Lexington, Massachusetts, on April 19, 1775, but the clash between American colonists and British soldiers is considered the historic beginning of the war for independence. In actuality, however, there were several earlier wars in the New World. Many of these battles formed a backdrop to conflicts that would lead to the Revolution. Many also gave a hint of the shifting alliances and struggles between and among various Native and European groups. At least one of these wars was fought over issues of freedom. Like the Revolution, it also involved British and American troops. But that is where the similarity ended.

On May 5, 1763, members of the Potawatomie, Huron, and Ottawa tribes gathered in a Potawatomie village near Fort Detroit to listen to the words of a great Ottawa chief. His name was Pontiac. He stepped to the center of the council ring and warned that the British were out to destroy the Natives. The goods they sold were overpriced and did not last, Pontiac said. The British commander laughed when Indians died and refused to help when they were sick.

Those in the council ring that night had been allies in the Seven Years' War against England — what was known as the French and Indian War. France lost that war in 1763, giving up most of its territory in North America. Pontiac now urged his brothers to rise up against the British on their own and drive them from Native lands.

Many American Indian nations did arise. All that spring and summer, warriors from more than a dozen tribes in the Great Lakes region attacked British forts in what came to be known as Pontiac's Uprising. In what could be considered the first American Revolution, Pontiac's troops captured eight British forts west of Fort Pitt (today's Pittsburgh).

But the British sent in more soldiers, and the Indians ran out of supplies; they also failed to capture the most important forts — Detroit, Niagara, and Pittsburgh. Equally important, the British killed Indian women and children and destroyed villages whenever the Indians resorted to their hit-and-run ambushes. In the fall of 1763, Pontiac's resistance collapsed.

A Land of Different People

The alliance of Indians brought together under Pontiac represented just a fraction of the hundreds of Native peoples and cultures across the North American continent. The America that was being settled by colonists also held an incredible variety of people from many social classes and backgrounds. There were slaves, servants, farmers, hunters, blacksmiths, carpenters, potters, weavers, seamstresses, ropemakers, sailors, laborers, schoolteachers, tavern owners, and more. There were unmarried women who farmed or held paying jobs and married women who worked long hours without pay as mothers and homemakers. And there were children — slaves, servants, apprentices, or assistants to their parents — who attended school whenever they could.

Recent arrivals from Africa had been brought to North America against their will as slaves. Many immigrants from European countries spoke no English, and only a few could read or write any language. They were poor, owning no property and having no vote in political affairs. A few were wealthy landowners, planters, merchants, publishers, lawyers, and other professionals who did vote and whose financial affairs would be seriously threatened by the restrictive laws imposed by England on the eve of the Revolution.

England's heavy-handed ways converted many of these struggling Americans from friends to enemies — in the space of a decade. In 1775, colonial America would find itself swept up in the Revolution. Because of different cultures and circumstances, not all citizens would view the conflict in the same way. They would act based on their interests and need to preserve their way of life. Some would fight for England; most would support the American cause; still others would remain neutral. All would find their lives changed permanently — for better or for worse — as a result of the war.

European Colonists, Rich and Poor

Colonial America was a land of opportunity for white males, especially those who were willing to enslave or exploit others. But not all European colonists were slave owners, not all treated Indians badly, and not many were rich. Many colonists were poor and isolated from the swirl of political and economic change going on in the colonies before the Revolution. It is important to realize that colonists at the time of the Revolution were a diverse, rapidly growing, and changing people.

White immigrants came mostly from England in the 1600s. But in the years leading up to the Revolution, more arrived from Switzerland, Germany, Ireland, and Scotland. There were also many Dutch in New York and French Huguenots (Protestants) in South Carolina and other colonies. Counting slaves, nearly half of all colonial people were no longer of English descent.

At the top of the social ladder in both the North and South were a few wealthy white men who owned enormous estates or plantations and dozens or hundreds of slaves. In New York, some of these men came from aristocratic families who secured their large land holdings through political connections. Others were newly arrived immigrants who, in colonies like Georgia and South Carolina, took advantage of cheap land and unpaid labor to amass quick fortunes.

In northern cities, men made money as merchants and ship owners. Like landowners, they used their money to influence government policies, but they did not hold absolute control. Unlike Europe, colonial America was an open society for white men. Many men owned land, and political leaders could arise from any class. John Adams, a Revolutionary leader who became the second U.S. president, was the son of a farmer. Benjamin Franklin and Alexander Hamilton were sons of poor men.

Whatever their background, the rich, who had everything to lose, and the poor, who had nothing to lose whatsoever, found themselves united against the British. Among the poorest were Irish and Scotch immigrants who moved into Pennsylvania and New Jersey from New England around 1770 as the economy in Massachusetts and elsewhere went sour. Like these poor Scottish and Irish Americans, many people who fought in the Revolution were recent immigrants without jobs or prospects.

Rural Life Dominates Colonial America. For most European colonists in the years leading to the Revolution, America was a rural society. The North was sprinkled with farming communities, each with a few hundred families who worked the land or provided services in town, usually without slaves. Farms were small. If a man owned fifty acres, he could keep his family secure and have something to pass on to his children.

A colonial settler hands out small amounts of corn to family members after a bad harvest. Many European settlers were farmers who lived a difficult, impoverished existence. Although their lives seemed far removed from problems in the cities that led to war with England, most of them united against the British.

In the South, there were also many small independent farmers and many other colonial men who labored on farms without owning land or slaves. South Carolina was the only colony in pre-Revolutionary times where most planters were wealthy slaveholders. Otherwise, only about 10 percent of the white men in the South owned large plantations with more than twenty slaves. However, most southern white men at the time dreamed of a plantation with hundreds of slaves, while northern colonists were abandoning slavery.

Diversity of City Life. Only about 4 percent of the colonial population lived in larger cities, where life was more competitive and stressful. None of the strict rules that governed business and trades in Europe applied in the New World. Opportunities arose as old ones dried up. Success went to those who could adapt to unstable and uncertain times.

Life was more ethnically and religiously diverse in northern cities. With thirty thousand people, Philadelphia was the largest city at the time of the Revolution. Its street signs were written in two languages — German and English — to aid the latest wave of European immigrants. Quakers founded Philadelphia and set its tone. Puritans predominated in Boston, but Catholics, Jews, and various Protestants worshiped freely in both cities. New York, with eighteen thousand people, was mostly Dutch and had the greatest number of slaves of any northern city. Charleston, South Carolina, with fourteen thousand people, was the smallest major city. Its wealthy merchants owned plantations, and more than half of the population were slaves.

Indentured Servants. European colonists lived in the cities as merchants, traders, and apprentices. Many other men, women, and children were indentured servants. In exchange for passage to America, plus food, shelter, and clothing once they arrived, indentured servants agreed to work for five or more years for whomever bought them on the auction block. Conditions were harsh — many servants died before they were freed; others found only poverty at the end of their service. But there were always enough successes to keep more hopeful indentured servants coming. Three of them — Daniel Dulany, Charles Thomson, and John Lamb — became revolutionary leaders.

Poverty Grows. Poverty increased after the French and Indian War as cities swelled with immigrants, injured veterans, and the unemployed. Poorhouses were filled and beggars were plentiful. In Boston in 1770, nearly one-third of the free adult men owned no property and lived in rented rooms or slept in the back of taverns. The 1770 Boston tax lists showed that 1 percent of the property owners owned 44 percent of the wealth. Throughout the colonies, 10 percent of the white men owned nearly half of the wealth and held 14 percent of the population as slaves. Since only those with property could vote, political decisions were made by the few.

Limits on Women's Rights

Marriage and motherhood were the primary goals for colonial women, and because men outnumbered them, most women did marry. Unlike American Indian women, white women did not retain legal rights after marriage. The man was the master of the household, and his wife had no legal or political recourse. Her husband controlled her property, and except in Connecticut, he controlled her children, too. He could send them where he pleased. Women were expected to devote themselves to homes, husbands, and children.

Unmarried women were looked down upon socially, but they had legal rights and could inherit and control their own property. The same was true for widows. Widows and unmarried women frequently ran farms, retail shops, or taverns, practiced trades, or took in lodgers for extra money.

Sexual equality was most nearly achieved by the Quakers, who formed a large part of the population in Pennsylvania and New Jersey and spoke out strongly against war and slavery. Quaker women were ministers at a time when almost no other religious denominations gave them a voice, and they held separate meetings to discuss personal and community problems. Quaker schools were marked by equal education for boys and girls.

A colonial woman loads a musket. Women often had to defend themselves on the frontier, and many on the patriot side used their weapons against British soldiers.

Children Sharing Adult Duties

European colonists expected adult behavior from their children. Sometimes this meant strict upbringing; at other times, it meant neglect or permissiveness. Children were prepared to be on their own at an early age. Girls per-

Women in trades

While married colonial women usually relied on their husbands for their economic welfare, their widowed and unmarried sisters frequently made important contributions in businesses and trades. In Baltimore, Betsy Ross was an upholsterer; Ann Rawlins was a plasterer; Mary Katherine Goddard was a printer who published the first copy of the Declaration of Independence to include the signers' names. In Boston, Mary Salmon was a blacksmith; Elizabeth Russell a coachmaker; and Sarah Jewell a ropemaker. Lydia Darragh of Philadelphia was an undertaker.

formed household duties, while boys helped on the farm and in the workshop or store. City children were more likely to attend school than were farm youngsters, and boys more than girls. Wealthy fathers often hired tutors to teach their sons and daughters at home. Some sent children to school in England or boarded them with a minister. Poor city children spent their days in the streets until hired as apprentices at the age of fourteen.

Whites Push Westward

European colonists were restless, forever pushing west. This urge westward had several causes: poor farming practices that quickly depleted land; the desire for larger farms to divide among sons; the wish for a better life by impoverished immigrants and unemployed city dwellers; and the hope for instant wealth by land speculators. A common thread among all such pioneers was the desire to be left alone.

As they moved west, most European settlers ignored American Indian claims to the land. Colonial governments purchased land illegally or tricked Indians into treaties that relinquished large portions for white settlement. Many European-Americans died in clashes with Native people over these lands. Others died of exposure, injury, disease, or other conditions brought on by the poverty and hardship of life on the frontier.

But nothing could stop the move west. If anything, England's Proclamation of 1763, which restricted white settlement to the area east of the Appalachian Mountains, made the pioneers more willing to rebel against the British, forcing many American Indians to join the British in the coming battle.

American Indians — Rich and Varied Cultures

On the eve of the Revolution, more than six hundred thousand American Indians, representing nearly six hundred tribal groups, lived in what is now the United States. Only a few thousand lived near the Atlantic Ocean in the region occupied by the thirteen English colonies that would become the United States. There had been many thousands of Natives in this region when white settlers first arrived, but by the late 1700s, many were dead from war or disease.

Most Natives who interacted with European settlers in the mid-1700s lived on the western frontiers of the colonies and in the vast region between the Appalachian Mountains and the Mississippi River. They were primarily farmers who also fished and hunted. They lived in settled communities. Of the dozens of tribes in this region, no two were exactly alike, but some shared similar languages and lifestyles.

Algonquian Share Common Customs. Algonquian-speaking Indians included the Ottawa, Menominee, Algonkin, Potawatomie, and some bands of Ojibway (Chippewa). They lived in what is now Michigan, Wisconsin, and Ontario, Canada. Along the prairies of what became Indiana, Illinois, southern Wisconsin, and Kentucky there were other Algonquians such as the Sauk, Fox, Kickapoo, Illinois, Miami, and Shawnee.

Algonquians grew corn, squash, and beans and lived in wigwams, dome-shaped huts made by placing bark and animal skins or woven mats over arched

poles. Families often banded together in large villages, which they surround-ed by a fence of tall, pointed poles called a palisade. Like other Indian groups, Algonquian-speaking tribes formed confederations, such as the Powhatan Con-federacy, which existed in the 1600s in Virginia and numbered thirty-two tribes and two hundred villages.

Six Nations of Iroquois. Iroquois-speaking tribes also formed confedera-tions. They had a well-organized and powerful alliance at the time of the Rev-olutionary War that dated from the late 1500s and had been formed to create peaceful relations among its original members — the Seneca, Cayuga, Ononda-ga, Oneida, and Mohawk. The alliance was called the League of the Iroquois or Five Nations, and its members lived throughout the woodlands of New York.

When the Tuscarora, who were originally from North Carolina, joined the League in 1722, it became known as the Six Nations. The Tuscarora had been driven north by war with British forces and other Indians. There were other Iroquois-speaking tribes that were not members of the League, such as the Huron, Neutral, Erie, and Tobacco of Ontario.

Iroquois from different families lived together in a dwelling called a long-house, which could be as much as one hundred feet in length. It consisted of a log frame usually covered with bark, with a door at either end. Down the center were fireplaces, and each family had its own apartment opposite a fire. Smoke drifted up through an opening in the roof that also let in light and could be covered with bark in bad weather.

This man displays a string of wampum to his friends. These col-orful sashes and belts made of beads or pol-ished shells served a wide variety of uses. Indians used them as money, ceremonial pledges, and orna-ments.

Two Seminoles launch a dugout canoe in the Florida Everglades. The Seminole, who long resisted compromise with colonial powers and the U.S. government alike, counted among their members slaves who had escaped from southern plantations.

The Iroquois League had a democratic system of government that was designed to keep the peace among member tribes and plan defenses against enemies. Fifty chiefs, or sachems, representing the six tribes met around a council fire. They were all men, but they were chosen by the older Iroquois women. Iroquois society was matrilineal, which meant the family line continued through the women, and women greatly influenced decisions.

Farmers of the Southeast. In the Southeast, the largest Native groups included the Cherokee, Choctaw, Chickasaw, Creek, and Seminole. They were farmers, and their traditional houses were made by weaving twigs around tall poles, then filling in the walls with a mixture of grass and clay. Sometimes

The custom for women

In 1762, Kanadiohora, a Seneca leader, told a British Indian agent, Sir William Johnson, that at the request of the Seneca women, he wished to speak to him. When Johnson told Kanadiohora not to bring women to the council meeting, the Seneca replied that it was the custom for women to be present at such occasions and that their presence was important to the men. Johnson won out. Yet he later married Molly Brant, whose brother Joseph Brant was a Mohawk leader. Molly's importance to her people increased Johnson's influence with them, and they remained loyal to the English for many years.

the houses were two stories high and divided into rooms. Seminoles in Florida lived in open-walled houses because of the hot weather.

Southeastern Indians were quick to adopt European ways, and so Europeans often called them the "Five Civilized Tribes." At the time of the Revolutionary War, for example, many Cherokee lived in log cabins in or near the Smoky Mountains. Like the Iroquois, southeastern Indians were matrilineal. In a Cherokee family, a father taught his son to hunt, but the child's maternal uncle was the disciplinarian — even though he lived in another household. In matrilineal tribes, women controlled all property.

Women and Children in Native Cultures

Native people looked to the land, waters, sky, and creatures around them for spiritual guidance, and these elements differed from one area to another. For these and other reasons, spiritual beliefs and practices varied among North America's many Native groups. Many spiritual lives were women-centered, however. For example, many Iroquoian people of the Northeast believed they came into the world from the mud on the back of the Earth, which they called Grandmother Turtle. The Cherokee of the southeast believed life began with Corn Mother.

Groups whose spiritual lives centered on women gave them a special place in everyday decision making. Iroquois and Cherokee women nominated the chiefs and subchiefs who ran their governments, and they could recall them if they were displeased. They were responsible for the distribution and use of food, and they were experts on growing and harvesting crops. Women sat at council meetings to represent other women and children.

As this painting illustrates, European men sometimes married Indian women and became members of their families. This painting also illustrates the fact that in many Native cultures, such as those of the Iroquois, women shared equal social footing with men and played a central role in political, cultural, and spiritual affairs.

Women in other tribes also were known to rush onto battlefields to protect injured husbands or brothers and as a result might later fight in other wars or receive war titles that allowed them to sing and dance with the other warriors. By the late 1700s, the status of American Indian women had lessened because European men did not recognize women as decision-makers or leaders.

American Indian children participated in tribe or village activities from an early age, often learning skills less by watching the adults than by trying to do the activities themselves. Parents seemed permissive by European standards. Yet children in most Native cultures were not allowed to fight, hurt, or ridicule others, and they learned to respect old people. European men sometimes married American Indian women. But other European men kidnapped and abused them and rewarded Indian men who brought them female slaves from other tribes. American Indian children also were sold into slavery. These slaves often were taken to the West Indies, where conditions were even worse than in the American colonies. Many died there from tropical and other diseases.

Indian Lands Threatened

Once the French and the Indians were defeated in the Seven Years' War, white settlers began moving onto land recently acquired by England. There were many bloody conflicts between Indians and white settlers over these lands. The English decided whites should live separately from Indians until an orderly way of settling the lands could be found. Unfortunately, the British were unable to enforce this decision. White expansion continued, leading to conflict and Indian land loss, and many Native people later refused to side with the colonists in the Revolution.

Africans Suffering under Slavery

There were about 2.5 million people living in the thirteen founding colonies at the time of the American Revolution. About five hundred thousand were Africans, and most — wherever they lived — were slaves. Slaves wanted freedom more than anything. But colonial society at the time considered most Africans to be property and passed laws forbidding escape or rebellion. Slaves

A superior social bond?

In the course of the Revolutionary War, colonial children were sometimes carried off to Indian villages. They were treated the same as Native children, and many liked their new lives so well that they refused to leave when their parents came looking for them after the war.

This caused Hector St. Jean Crevecoeur, a French writer, to observe, "There must be in [the American Indian] a social bond something singularly captivating and far superior to anything to be boasted of among us; for thousands of Europeans are Indians, and we have no examples of even one of those [Indians] having from choice become European."

could not own weapons and were not allowed to testify in court against white people. In the southern colonies, where they sometimes outnumbered colonists, slaves could not gather in groups or leave the plantation without permission.

Although life was difficult everywhere for African slaves, conditions were worse in the South because slavery was tied to the agricultural economy. Owners put their concern for crops above concern for human life. They tried to get all the work they could from their slaves. On large plantations, crops such as tobacco, cotton, and rice required grueling hand labor that sometimes led to disease or death. Slaves were often beaten or punished severely if they did not work hard or if they disobeyed. Slaves might even be disciplined by white children they had helped raise.

There were far fewer slaves in the northern colonies — about 3 to 10 percent of the total population — and they were generally treated better. They worked as craftspeople, farm hands, or personal servants and usually ate, slept, and lived in their master's house. In the North, slavery was more common in the cities than in the countryside. By the middle of the eighteenth century, more than 15 percent of the population of New York City was Black, most of them slaves.

Northern slave owners were more willing than southern slave owners to send slave children to school. They also encouraged adult slaves to attend church. Perhaps the hardest part about northern slave life was the isolation of slaves, who usually lived singly or in pairs in white homes. In the South, slaves typically worked in groups and lived in their own quarters on farms and plantations with from ten to fifty or even a hundred other slaves.

Southern slaves, then, had a greater chance to be away from their owners and develop their own sense of family, community life, and culture. Many slaves had been born in the colonies by the time of the Revolutionary War. Others were born in Africa and brought with them strong memories of a rich and varied heritage, which they shared.

African Origins. African slaves came to America primarily from West and Central Africa. Some had been slaves in Africa, but it was a different form of slavery that often reflected social status. Slavery in Africa was not based on economics as it was in the New World. In most African systems, slaves enjoyed the right to marry, earn income,

A group of African slaves works the fields on a tobacco plantation in a southern colony. The intolerable conditions under which slaves lived and worked in the South, as well as the very existence of slavery in the South, were tied directly to the South's agricultural economy.

African culture in the colonies

One of the ways Africans kept their culture alive under slavery was through architecture. In coastal regions of the South, they built their houses out of tabby, a mixture of lime and seashells used along the Guinea coast of West Africa. The slaves also used tabby to construct walls, fences, roadways, and even their owners' houses, and thus African culture affected the lives of white people in colonial America as well. Round houses with steeply pitched roofs were also popular with some southern slaves, as they had been in Africa. These houses stayed cooler because the circular shape helped distribute the sun's heat more evenly. European colonists borrowed this concept for many of their structures, such as icehouses.

hold property, gain wealth, and even inherit the master's property. Most Ashanti slaves, for instance, eventually were adopted into the owner's family, and their descendants lived freely.

African slaves represented hundreds of ethnic groups and spoke more than one hundred languages. There were common sounds and patterns in many of their languages, however, that helped them communicate with each other. Some slaves kept up the African tradition of developing a language their masters could not understand. In South Carolina, for instance, slaves from the Congo-Angola region created a language called Gullah, a mix of African and English words.

The Importance of Family. Slave and free alike, Africans in America shared a sense of kinship and family solidarity. In Africa, families were the basis of social life. Extended families were common and included grandparents, uncles, aunts, cousins, the unborn, and the dead, who still existed in the memories of living relatives. In some African societies, a man might have more than one wife. Each mother lived in a separate hut with her children, and everyone was united by their relationship with the same husband or father.

Since slaves in the colonies went where their owners sent them, slavery could ruin family life. Adults were often separated from their older children and elderly parents, and husbands frequently were torn from their wives. Slaves had no legal right to marry in America, but they still valued marriage. They created their own marriage ceremonies, often based on African customs. In North Carolina, for example, it was common for a man to make the woman a present, such as a brass ring. If she accepted the ring, she became his wife. If they decided to part, she returned the ring.

African-American Women and Children

In African societies, a woman's main purpose was to have and raise children. Motherhood was a key duty for African women in America, too. But slavery separated women from parts of their culture that gave their lives meaning. As new mothers, slaves were expected to work, and they could be whipped if they did not get enough done. Because they were often forced to raise their children without the partnership and protection of their husbands, female slaves forged strong bonds with one another, developing a firm sense of womanhood. Many slave women worked in the fields alongside the men, performing labor considered too difficult or inappropriate for white women.

Slave children grew up among themselves, as most adult slaves were off in the fields all day. In preparation for future roles, boys and girls did the same type of work. They watched babies, tended livestock, hauled water to the field hands, and performed kitchen and housekeeping chores. Girls played the same games as boys — tag, marbles, or running through the woods climbing trees. By the time they were twelve years old, most slaves were assigned fulltime adult chores. Such hardship may have made the boys more ready for the rigors of military service than were the sons of American colonists at the time of the Revolution.

A Religious People

As slaves, most Africans remained committed to their spiritual values, even though traditional religious practices were forbidden by owners who considered these activities "heathen" and feared religious teachings might feed the desire to rebel. At the time of the Revolution and beyond, some slaves practiced religious rituals in secret.

Eventually, Blacks accepted Protestant Christianity, which they mixed with West African traditions. For instance, West Africans saw death as a journey from the world of the living to the world of spirits. As Christians, Americans of African descent held funerals that included dancing, singing, and rejoicing. They also blended African rhythm patterns into Anglo-American melodies to create spirituals that allowed them to express their deepest sorrows and pain while singing of their sense of self-worth and desire for freedom.

By the time of the American Revolution, Christianity had become increasingly important to slaves because it spoke to them of brotherhood and freedom from oppression. Many slave owners in the South were reluctant to let slaves attend church and did so only after missionaries promised that slaves would learn meekness and obedience. Slaves, however, found in Christianity the hope that they would some day be free.

The Desire for Freedom Prevails

Only about 4 percent of the Black population was free by the decade leading up to the American Revolution. Some were runaways who had managed to avoid capture. Others were freed by their masters or were descendants of indentured servants who had served out their debt and earned their independence. Some managed to buy their own freedom. In the South, free Blacks were usually farm hands or farmers. In northern and southern cities, they worked in textile mills, tobacco plants, and shipyards.

Some escaped to remote areas, such as Florida, which was at the time a Spanish colony. Protected by swampland and unsettled frontier, they lived among Seminoles and other local Indians, often intermarrying with them. They farmed, establishing their own government in what came to be known as Maroon settlements, from the French word *marron*, which means "runaway Black slave." Often, they were able to defend themselves from recapture by white slave owners and live independently for years.

There was considerable resistance to slavery, even though few Blacks were free at the time of the Revolution. In fact, most slaves were aware of the colonial struggle for political liberties, and this made them more eager for freedom than ever.

This an artist's view of the Battle of Lexington, where the Revolution officially began in April 1775. More than seventy minutemen faced down the British in Lexington and in the neighboring Massachusetts village of Concord. At least nine of these able volunteers were Black.

CHAPTER THREE

Unleashing Freedom's Cry

Despite the nearly complete lack of freedom in their lives in colonial America, Black people were forced to choose sides in the Revolutionary conflict. Whereas colonists might have been restless over their economic grievances with England, slaves wanted only the kinds of liberty and equality a revolution might bring. At least five thousand Black men, slave and free, fought on the American side, most of them from the North. Many, especially in New England, where the abolitionist movement was strongest, hoped the war would bring a better life.

Unfortunately, most colonists did not believe the fight for political freedom had anything to do with the personal freedom of Africans. Thousands of slaves in the South, seeing no other route to liberty, took up arms for England because the British promised them freedom. Such choices in the early years of the war had a marked effect on Black and white people alike.

Blacks at Lexington and Concord

The Revolutionary War began on April 19, 1775, in the villages of Lexington and Concord, Massachusetts, when British troops attempted to seize American powder and weapons. They were met first in Lexington by a small band of soldiers known as minutemen, so called because they were volunteers who could fight with a minute's notice. The minutemen had been warned the night before that the British were coming, thanks to Paul Revere's famous ride from Boston.

At least nine Blacks were among the seventy-some minutemen who faced the British. Prince Easterbrooks, a Lexington slave, was one of the first wounded. Later, he served in most major campaigns of the war. Peter Salem, a slave from Framingham, Massachusetts, also helped push the British back and two months later was one of twenty Black people who fought outside Boston at Bunker Hill.

Bunker Hill Heroes

This painting depicts the Battle of Bunker Hill, the bloodiest of the war. At the far right is Peter Salem, credited with killing a British commander in the fight. Salem was a Massachusetts slave and one of some five thousand Blacks who fought on the patriot side throughout the Revolution.

Bunker Hill, which took place on June 17, 1775, was the bloodiest battle of the entire war, with more than one thousand British and more than four hundred colonists killed or wounded before they ran out of ammunition and fled. To save ammunition, the legend goes, colonists had been ordered not to shoot at the British until they saw "the whites of their eyes." Peter Salem, the slave from Massachusetts, must have taken very careful aim because he is credited with killing the British commander, Major John Pitcairn. Because of this deed, Salem was later presented to George Washington as a hero. He was also portrayed in a famous painting, *The Battle of Bunker Hill.*

Salem Poor, a free Black man who left his wife at home to join the fight, was another hero at Bunker Hill. He is believed to have killed another British leader, Lieutenant Colonel James Abercrombie. Poor stayed in the army for years but was never publicly rewarded for his heroism, despite the fact that fourteen American officers petitioned the Massachusetts Court to recognize him.

The battle for Bunker Hill was part of a seige to free Boston from British control. The seige forced the British to depart Boston on March 17, 1776. Patriots were less fortunate in New York, as the British landed a huge force on Long Island later that same year and pushed George Washington and his new Continental Army from Brooklyn into Manhattan, then north and finally west across the Delaware River. Washington boosted colonial American morale on

Christmas Day, 1776, by crossing the Delaware and defeating British forces at Trenton, New Jersey.

Slavery as a War Issue in the South

The conflict took a different turn in the South, where it focused on slavery. There were 450,000 slaves in the South in 1775; in some areas, they outnumbered whites. Slave unrest increased considerably in the months after Lexington and Concord, alarming the South's white population. Colonial soldiers patrolled the streets of Charleston and in other towns searched Black people's homes for guns and ammunition. In July, several North Carolina slaves were arrested hours before they carried out a plot to kill slave owners. They had been promised freedom by British commanders if their rebellion succeeded. In August, a free Black man named Thomas Jeremiah was executed in Charleston for planning to aid the British navy while freeing slaves.

Several Black preachers in South Carolina, all slaves and two of them women, were accused of plotting a rebellion against their wealthy owners at about the same time. Slave owners in Georgia were so frightened that they tried to kill a Black preacher who — like Phillis Wheatley, a slave who became famous as a poet — compared slaves to the Biblical Israelites. A white planter helped the preacher escape.

In stirring the hopes of freedom-hungry slaves, England hoped to convince southern slave owners that they had too much to lose by going to war. Instead, England's actions made many slave owners even more anti-British. Slave owners also reacted by treating slaves more brutally; those caught plotting were usually killed as examples to others.

When England could not control the South, it tried other tactics. In November of 1775, Lord Dunmore, the British governor of Virginia, promised freedom to slaves who joined the British side. Thousands accepted his offer. In the coming months, hundreds more slaves fled plantations and farms along the coast of Georgia to board British warships to fight for the king.

A Black soldier's bravery

"The Subscribers beg leave to report to Your Honorable House (which we do in justice to the character of so brave a Man) that under Our Own observation, We declare that a Negro Man, Called Salem Poor of Col. Frye's Regiment, Captain Ames Company, in the late Battle at Charlestown, behaved like an Experienced Officer, as well as an excellent Soldier, to Set Forth Particulars of his Conduct would be Tedious. We would only beg leave to say in the Person of this sd [sic] Negro centors [sic] a Brave and gallant soldier, the reward to so great and Distinguished a Character, we submit to the Congress."

— From a letter dated December 1, 1775, to the General Court of Massachusetts suggesting that the Continental Congress reward Salem Poor for his valor. It was signed by two colonels, one lieutenant colonel, and twelve other officers. Despite the letter, there is no record that Poor was ever honored.

Following a defeat in Charleston at the hands of colonists under General Charles Lee in 1776, the British suspended operations in the South for two years. Focusing on campaigns outside of the South, British forces retook Fort Ticonderoga in northern New York early in 1777. It had been in patriot hands since Ethan Allen, Benedict Arnold, and a group of patriots known as the Green Mountain Boys stormed the fort in 1775. England would also have its hands full on other fronts and with other rivals. On the high seas, for example, France would send a fleet of ships to aid the struggling Americans in 1778. Aid followed from Spain in 1779 and from Holland in 1780.

Continental Army Excludes Slaves

The issue of Blacks in the military was a topic of discussion at the Second Continental Congress, which opened in May 1775. Until that time, the colonies had no standing armies. They relied on volunteers to fight at Lexington, Concord, and in other early battles. Volunteer militiamen typically served for short periods. Most were ill trained. So Congress established the Continental Army, appointing George Washington to lead it.

Blacks had been accepted in military service during previous wars with Indians, and slaves who served often were given their freedom. Although slaves fought in the early battles of the Revolution, the new American leaders had second thoughts about their participation once slave revolts loomed in the South. Many leaders were slave owners who would never accept Black people as equals if treated with respect.

Five days after his appointment as commander in chief, George Washington issued orders against enlisting Black recruits, although he allowed those already in military service to stay. Later, when it looked as if this policy would convince people of color to join the other side, Washington changed his mind. However, he still refused to let slaves enlist, for fear they might mutiny. Only free people of color could join the army.

By 1777, however, there was a shortage of white volunteers. Most colonies began accepting slaves to fill quotas imposed by the Continental Congress. Rhode Island attracted 250 men by offering slaves their freedom. Connecticut created an all-African company in which free Blacks and slaves fought together. Several colonies passed laws allowing slaves to fight in the place of owners who were called to serve. Some owners offered their slaves freedom in exchange for their service. Eventually, Blacks were fighting alongside whites in almost every American regiment. Though few slaves were promised freedom, they pursued freedom when the war ended.

Many Reasons to Rebel

Patriotism was one reason that white men fought on the American side, but it was not the only reason. In addition to southerners who took up arms because they were afraid England would free their slaves, some colonists were lured by personal gain. Poor farmers and indentured servants saw the military as a place where they might rise in rank, make a little money, and improve their social status.

William Scott of Petersborough, New Hampshire, turned down the military's request that he enlist as a private. Scott asked for and got an appointment as a lieutenant colonel. "If my captain were killed," he reasoned, "I should rise in rank and should still have a chance to rise higher. These, Sir," he said after he was wounded at Bunker Hill, "were the only Motives of my entering the Service."

Some joined at the promise of owning land, as was the case with tenant farmers in Dutchess County, New York. Many had complained that the pay for privates was low compared to that of officers. In response, the New York legislature passed a bill that confiscated land from wealthy men who remained loyal to England (Loyalists) and divided it among those who would enlist.

Some joined for adventure or to avenge the deaths of loved ones. Still others became soldiers after colonies passed draft laws. These draft laws meant forced military service for most colonial men, but they were barely an inconvenience to those who could afford to pay substitutes to fight. This angered poor people, who could not afford stand-ins. In Boston, there was rioting when the draft law was announced.

On the frontier, men and women alike fought to protect their homes and property more than to uphold political ideals far removed from their rugged lives. Frontier law enforcement was weak, and many men ignored orders to fight in distant areas. Some on the frontier remained neutral, including several thousand men in western North Carolina known as the Regulators. They were poor white farmers who, in the 1760s, spoke out against high local taxes. Because neither colonial legislators nor the governor appointed by England promised tax relief, most were unwilling to side with either the colonies or the Crown.

Life in the Continental Army

Life in the Continental Army, like most armies, meant days and even weeks of boring routine, training, and marching, broken up by minutes or perhaps an hour of fighting using a variety of weapons. Colonial soldiers fought with rifles whose accuracy was often unreliable, cannon that fired deadly buckshotlike pellets called grapeshot, swords and knives, and even bare hands in desperate situations.

Game was plentiful and supplemented jerky, cornmeal, oats, and other food. Fresh fruits and vegetables were either picked as the troops moved or were simply not in the diet. Rum was stored in a barrel, perhaps carried on an ox cart, and was consumed on a daily basis.

Soldiers slept on bedrolls they cinched to their belts. Also on the belt were containers for gunpowder (sometimes a cow's horn), wadding for keeping the powder in place, lead shot, gun-cleaning supplies, and a ramrod; tobacco and a pipe; and assorted provisions, mementos, and a purse. Troops went for weeks without a bath or a change of clothing. Northern forces sometimes were sewn into long underwear in November, not emerging until it was warm enough in the spring to bathe in a creek!

More than half of those who were wounded died of their wounds. If the bullet or blade failed to kill them, infection easily could. Anesthetics were unknown, so whiskey and rum were the only painkillers; the suffering must have been incredible. Amputations were performed without anesthesia, using the sharpest knife available as the wounded soldier was held down by several other troops. Sometimes, when a gangrenous limb was cut off, it was subsequent bleeding, and not the infection, that killed the patient.

American Indians Caught in the Middle — Again

For American Indians, the Revolution may have seemed a matter of choosing between the lesser of two evils. Most Natives along the frontier sided with France rather than with England in the Seven Years' War because France was less eager to acquire Indian land. Here was another big war between white people, and this time England, rather than the American colonists, seemed the smaller threat.

When the Revolution started, both sides tried to keep Indians out of the fight. England thought the war would be short and that it was a matter of quieting disturbances in and around Boston. The British did not want to spend money to arm Indians. They were also afraid that colonists who had not made up their minds to rebel against England would do so if attacked by Indians. Meanwhile, colonists tried to convince Indians along the western frontier to stay neutral because they knew that if the Natives fought for anyone, it would be for England.

In 1775, the Continental Congress established a department to handle Indian affairs, much like the department England operated for years. Congress appointed commissioners to head this department, which promised Indians that land rights as set forth in the Proclamation of 1763 and later treaties would be honored permanently.

Most Indians were not eager to fight. They knew from past experience that being in the middle of a white man's fight rarely worked to their advantage.

Joseph Brant (Thayendanegea), the famous Mohawk leader, once had his portrait painted in Europe. Brant had close alliances with the British and encouraged his people to take their side in the war.

Seven hundred Iroquois met with American negotiators and then with each other in council; they agreed to "keep the hatchet buried deep" — to keep the peace — as long as their territory was respected. American agents held meetings in the South with the Creek and Cherokee. As the war continued, however, both sides realized they were fighting for control of the frontier and that they needed Indian support.

Split Loyalties among the Iroquois. Most Iroquois rallied behind Chief Thayendanegea, a Mohawk leader also known as Joseph Brant. Brant was loyal to the British. He had been in England with British Indian official Guy Johnson when the Iroquois promised colonists they would remain neutral. Returning to America in 1776, he slipped through American lines in New York and traveled northward to Iroquois territory, urging his people to support the British.

Joseph Brant, Mohawk leader

Thayendanegea, also known as Joseph Brant, was a Mohawk chief with deep-rooted British loyalty. As a boy he became a friend of Sir William Johnson, the British official for Indian affairs in the Northeast. Johnson married Molly Brant, Joseph's sister. Brant fought alongside Johnson in the French and Indian War in 1755 at the age of thirteen.

Johnson sent Brant to an American school, and he became the first Mohawk to read and write English. He also spoke several Indian languages and served as an interpreter for Sir William and is nephew, Guy Johnson. Sir William died in 1774.

When the war began a year later, Brant was in England with Guy Johnson, serving as his secretary and deputy. Brant became a celebrity in England. He had his portrait painted by a famous artist and was received by King George III. He obtained royal promises that Iroquois land rights would be guaranteed. Returning to America, he encouraged the Iroquois to fight for the British. All but the Oneida and Tuscarora did.

Cunneshote, also known as Stalking Turkey, was one of several Cherokee leaders who traveled to London in 1762 at the invitation of the Queen of England. Many Indians believed that the British were more reliable allies than the colonists, who seemed determined to ignore agreements struck between England and Indian nations over the sovereignty of Native lands.

The Iroquois remained neutral until the Americans broke a promise a year later by invading Mohawk territory. Following Brant's advice, most Iroquois backed the British. However, some Oneida and Tuscarora (also members of the Six Nations of the Iroquois Confederacy) sided with the colonists. They had been persuaded by missionaries from the Presbyterian Church, which was strongly anti-British.

The American Revolution thus turned members of the Six Nations against each other in a bloody civil war. The war would ruin the Iroquois Confederacy, bringing destruction to its lands.

Southeast Indians Support the British. In May 1776, the British sent Shawnee, Delaware, and Mohawk warriors south to preach war to the Cherokee, Creek, Choctaw, and Chickasaw. It did not take much to provoke the Cherokee who were angry about white settlements on their land. That summer, they attacked American settlements in Virginia, Georgia, and the Carolinas with arms supplied by the British. These southern colonies organized large armies that destroyed Cherokee villages and crops and forced the Cherokee into treaties that gave up portions of land. The Cherokee continued fighting the colonists for several years, however. The Choctaw and Creek helped the British in areas near the Mississippi River. The Chickasaw carried out raids against settlers as far north as Kentucky.

A British sympathizer, or Tory, is drummed out of his village because of his politics. Many people throughout the colonies opposed the break with England and were often persecuted by their neighbors.

War on the Northwest Frontier. It was like Pontiac's Uprising in reverse on the Northwest frontier, as Wyandot, Shawnee, Delaware, and other tribes helped the British protect their forts from assault by American colonists. British forces in turn helped Indians attack colonial settlements. The British commander at Detroit was known among Indians as the "Hair Buyer" because he paid for rebel scalps. Fighting raged on the frontier until the end of the war, putting men, women, and children — Native and colonial alike — in constant danger. An important victory for rebels came in 1779 when forces under George Roger Clark captured the fort at Vincennes in what is now Indiana.

Colonists on the British Side

Throughout the thirteen colonies there were American colonists who opposed the Revolution. These people came from many social and ethnic backgrounds. Some were rich; others were modest farmers or tradespeople. Many were against the Stamp Act, Townshend Acts, and the laws that closed down the Boston port in 1775. But for various reasons — economic, political, religious — they did not feel a need for independence. These people were known as Loyalists or Tories.

The greatest number of Loyalists lived in Georgia, the newest colony, which depended greatly on England for financial assistance. The Middle Colonies — New York, Pennsylvania, Delaware, and New Jersey — also had large numbers of Loyalists. These colonies had less industry than New England, so they were less affected by new British laws restricting business. Those who lived on the frontiers looked to England for protection from Indian attack. The Middle Colonies were also the most diverse ethnically and religiously, so it was less likely that the opinions of any one group would dominate.

New England, on the other hand, had a sense of unity fostered by town meetings and the Congregational Church, which many attended. New England's economy had the most to lose under the new tax laws, and it had more supporters of the American cause than any other region. However, there were many Loyalists in Massachusetts, especially among the oldest families.

New York City in flames

One of the worst civilian disasters took place in New York City ten weeks after the Declaration of Independence was adopted. On the night of September 20, 1776, a fire broke out and spread rapidly up Broadway through flimsily built, closely placed buildings. According to some accounts, the fire was set by patriots in foolish revenge for the fact that British troops had seized the city. Many people died in the fire, and five hundred homes were destroyed, more than one-fourth of the city.

A British officer described this terrible scene: "The sick, the aged, women, and children, half naked were seen going they knew not where, and taking refuge in houses which were at a distance from the fire, but from whence in several instances driven a second and even a third time by the devouring element, and at last in a state of despair, laying themselves down on the common."

Neighbor Against Neighbor

Thousands of Loyalist men fought for the British during the war. The conflict resembled a civil war, pitting neighbors and friends against each other. A Swiss-born stocking weaver named Peter Etter was a Loyalist and a close friend of John Adams; the war destroyed their friendship. Rebels often persecuted Loyalist minorities. They destroyed or confiscated property, beat them, and threatened their lives. In some towns, Loyalists were hanged. In 1775, Etter and his family fled their Massachusetts home.

A doomed, yet gifted, poet

"In every human breast, God has implanted a Principle, which we call love of freedom; it is impatient of Oppression, and pants for Deliverance; and by the leave of our modern Egyptians I will assert that the same Principle lives in us."

The words belong to Phillis Wheatley, an African slave who became world famous around 1770 as a poet. Wheatley's talents were discovered by her Boston owners, who bought her off a slave ship in 1761 when she was eight years old. The Wheatleys schooled Phillis, giving her time to write poems and read them in the homes of important Boston families. When she was nineteen, they helped her publish a book of poems, the first ever by an African-American woman, and sent her to England to promote it.

Wheatley often wrote poems about famous people. In 1775, she wrote a poem praising George Washington, who had been chosen to prepare the Continental Army for war by being named its commander in chief. Phillis sent the poem to George Washington. He was so impressed that he invited her to visit him at his headquarters in Cambridge, Massachusetts, which she did. By some accounts, he spent half an hour with her and treated her like a celebrity.

The words "modern Egyptians" in the lines above may have more than one meaning. Did Phillis see American slaveholders as "modern Egyptians," with Africans as the enslaved Israelites? Or were the British "modern Egyptians" who enslaved the colonists? Regardless, she knew that the Israelites eventually found freedom by reaching the Promised Land.

Wheatley identified with the patriot cause and looked to the Revolution as a way to win freedom for Americans of all races. Wheatley received her freedom in 1778 when her master died. Interest in her poetry declined, however, perhaps because her genteel style did not appeal to a nation at war. In 1784, Wheatley died in poverty at age thirty-one, just a few days before her poem celebrating the end of the war was printed.

Like Etter, many Loyalists became refugees. They sought protection in British-occupied cities. Thousands went to New York City, which the British held for most of the war. Conditions there became crowded, and food and firewood were scarce; many poor people were homeless. Other Loyalists went to British bases in Canada or Florida, where the men became soldiers. Families often fled together, sometimes taking slaves with them. Sometimes men left alone, hoping their wives would protect their property until the war ended.

But the fighting went on for eight years, much longer than the British expected, and many Loyalist women and children made difficult journeys on their own to find their husbands and fathers. Others switched sides. As the war continued, smaller and smaller numbers of Loyalists were willing to take up arms. They preferred being evacuated from places such as Savannah, in what is now Georgia, rather than continue fighting kin and neighbors. They were resettled in Canada, the West Indies, and elsewhere.

Women and the War

Life was difficult for women of all backgrounds and beliefs during the Revolution. Food and other goods were scarce. Prices skyrocketed. Disease spread quickly in cities crowded with refugees, and in September 1776, a disastrous fire struck New York City. People went about their daily lives as best they could.

Colonial women took care of their children while trying to maintain farms and businesses in the absence of husbands and fathers. Others earned livings as weavers, carpenters, blacksmiths, or shipbuilders. Some made extra money sewing uniforms and knitting stockings for the soldiers, or they turned their homes into hospitals for the wounded. Women survived best who could make their own cloth and grow their own food. At home and at work, they became decision-makers, learning authority.

Phillis Wheatley, the African-American poet, struggled consistently during the war. After being freed, she married John Peters, also a free Black. He practiced various trades but could not find steady work in war-torn Boston. She moved in with a relative of her former owner and worked in the home school this woman ran. She published another book of poetry, but people did not have money for such luxuries, and it sold few copies. Wheatley had two children, but there was no money for medical care, and they died as babies. She and her husband never made enough money to live together. She died as a cleaning woman in an African-American boardinghouse.

War Uproots Many. Women and children often fled their cities and villages or took shelter in cellars or stockades when armies approached. Margaret Hill Morris, a young Quaker widow opposed to violence, kept a diary during the war. In December 1776, she told how colonial troops fired on her town of Burlington, New Jersey, one afternoon because Tory soldiers had taken shelter there. Houses were damaged that day, but fortunately, she wrote, "Not one living creature, man or beast, was killed or wounded." On January 1, 1777, after weeks of heavy fighting in the area, she wrote, "This New Year's Day has not been ushered in with the usual ceremonies and rejoicing; indeed, I believe it will be the beginning of a sorrowful year to very many people."

Molly Pitcher carried water to patriot troops and became a gunner at the Battle of Monmouth when her husband fell. Many women followed their men to the front and found themselves facing the enemy on the battlefield. They also served as nurses, laundresses, and cooks.

Morris knew a lot about medicine and herbal remedies. There was no licensed doctor in Burlington during the war and so people depended on her skills. Every morning, a carriage came to her door and took her to see sick or wounded soldiers lodged in area homes. She also treated local citizens with smallpox and other illnesses. Medical supplies were scarce, so Morris secured ingredients from friends in nearby Philadelphia and opened a small pharmacy.

Women on the Battlefield. Hundreds of colonial women — some of them wives — followed the Continental Army, serving as nurses, laundresses, cooks, and companions. The British also had female followers, some of them carrying children in their arms and supplies on their backs. As the war continued, Black women were increasingly among this group; they were former slaves who had taken advantage of chaotic circumstances to escape from their owners. White Loyalist women and older girls were sometimes sent to frontier posts with their men to do housekeeping in exchange for their keep.

Some women crossed onto the battlefield during the war. Margaret Corbin took over her husband's cannon post when he was killed and kept firing until she herself was wounded. Molly Pitcher carried water to rebel troops and also became a gunner when her husband fell. Deborah Sampson disguised herself as a man at age twenty-two and actually enlisted in the Continental Army under the name Robert Shurtleff. An unidentified Cherokee woman was found among the dead by American soldiers after a fierce battle in 1776. Her face was painted like a male warrior's, and she was armed with a bow and arrow.

War Endangers Children

Childhood ended early during the war. Colonial boys were eligible to fight at age sixteen, and some joined even earlier. Children of all ages were affected by the war, as even the simplest activities became filled with danger. Many died, innocent victims of battle, hunger, and disease. During fighting in Trenton, New Jersey, a little girl was hit by cannon fire as she opened the door to her house. She was lucky, however, because while the shot knocked the comb out of her hair, it only grazed her skin. Children were routinely stopped and questioned by American officers in embattled areas. In her diary, Margaret Hill Morris related that an American officer once threatened to shoot her small son as a spy because he lingered too long around the military boats docked near the Morris home along the Delaware River.

Dicey Langston, at sixteen, carried messages to her brothers' patriot regiment in a region of South Carolina that was mostly Loyalist. Once, after she had warned the Americans of a pending attack, Loyalists decided to kill her elderly father in revenge. Dicey stood between her father and the pointed gun. The men retreated, not willing to kill a girl.

Seno and Titus were twelve-year-old twins for whom the war meant a chance at freedom. They were among a group of Georgia slaves who fled their plantation in 1780 to reach British lines. Many Black children, in fact, escaped toward freedom with their parents and other adults later in the war. As we will see, freedom became a reality after the war for many of these hopeful people.

In this illustration, George Washington is shown chatting amicably with a group of American Indians. This portrayal underscores the complex relationships among various Indian groups, the British, and colonists such as Washington, who led a ferocious military campaign against the Iroquois and encouraged western settlement on Indian lands.

CHAPTER FOUR

The War Drags On (1776 to 1780)

"We hold these truths to be self evident, that all men are created equal, that they are endowed by their Creator with certain unalienable rights, that among these are life, liberty, and the pursuit of happiness. That to secure these rights, Governments are instituted among Men, deriving their just powers from the consent of the governed, that whenever any Form of Government becomes destructive of these ends, it is the Right of the People to alter or to abolish it, and to institute new Government." — From the Declaration of Independence, adopted by the Continental Congress, July 4, 1776.

In the summer of 1776, while the Founding Fathers were discussing the wording of the Declaration of Independence, Cherokee warriors attacked isolated forts and settlements in Tennessee, Virginia, the Carolinas, and Georgia. They used guns supplied by the British, who urged them on against the settlers. The Cherokee did not care about the political struggle between the colonists and England, but they did care about their land and their survival. Led by Chief Dragging Canoe, they fought fiercely.

Nancy Ward, a relative of Chief Dragging Canoe, also was a leader among her people. They called her Beloved Woman because, years before, in a battle between Cherokees and Creeks, she fought bravely with her husband's rifle after he was killed. Ward was head of the Council of Women of her tribe and as such voted in the Chief's Council, could speak her opinion on all tribal matters, and had the right to decide the fate of captives.

Though she was a fighter, Ward also believed in peace, believing it best if her people and the settlers could learn to live side by side. When Chief Dragging Canoe attacked white settlements, she sent a warning to settlers so they could defend themselves. She also helped spare the lives of captured settlers, which was one of her privileges. One captive, a woman named Mrs. William Bean, was saved by Ward as she was about to be set afire.

Colonial troops struck back harshly against the Cherokee. They organized large militia armies that destroyed Cherokee villages and crops. At one point, the chiefs sent Ward to meet the advancing American troops to negotiate peace. She was unsuccessful. The war between the Cherokee and the colonists went on for two years. Because of widespread respect for Ward, the colonists spared her village in southern Tennessee. Nonetheless, the Cherokee lost much land. In 1780, two years after most Cherokee stopped fighting, North Carolina militiamen destroyed Cherokee villages and demanded more land.

"All Men Are Created Equal"

The men who signed the Declaration of Independence were not maliciously slighting women by omitting them from this important document. These men were products of their time, never realizing that women should have a voice in government. As we have seen, however, women of all races and ethnic backgrounds played important, often heroic roles in the American Revolution.

Blacks and American Indians also were overlooked in the Declaration's reference to the "consent of the governed." Slave or free, neither could vote in colonial America. Again, the omission reflects the ruling white-male attitude at the time. The Declaration condemned King George III for encouraging slaves and Indians alike to rise up against colonists: "He has excited domestic insurrection amongst us, and has endeavoured to bring on the inhabitants of our frontier. . . ."

Originally, the Declaration of Independence included a paragraph written by Thomas Jefferson condemning the slave trade. After much debate, however, the Continental Congress took the paragraph out when many southern

Early American leaders gather to sign the Declaration of Independence. Its message about equality and inalienable rights was applauded then and has remained a key aspect of the American heritage.

Thomas Jefferson talks to one of his slaves at his Virginia home, Monticello. Jefferson, who helped write the Declaration of Independence, spoke out against slavery yet owned many slaves. It was a contradiction he struggled with for much of his life.

delegates — and some northern delegates, as well — refused to sign the document unless the paragraph was dropped. Yet there was growing sentiment against slavery at the time, and despite its exclusive language, many Blacks, slave and free alike, were heartened by the Declaration. Hadn't these white men proclaimed to the world that "all men were created equal," and — with the understanding that in those days "men" meant "people" — weren't Blacks also men?

The Declaration's fiery cries for liberty caused hundreds of slaves to enlist on the colonists' side, taking last names like Freedom, Freeman, and Liberty. Though freedom was not always a condition of enlistment, many bargained for it anyway. For instance, Cato Freeman of Andover, Massachusetts, enlisted with the stipulation that, instead of the usual cash bounty offered to new recruits, he would receive "freedom in three years." The Declaration also encouraged more slaves in the North to petition local governments for freedom, and it caused many humanitarian white people to work for slavery's end.

State Antislavery Actions

After the Declaration of Independence was adopted, the colonies declared themselves states. They elected legislatures, which drew up constitutions. A weak central government created by the Continental Congress under the Articles of Confederation, which preceded the Constitution, would hold the thirteen states together. Delegates gave more power to the states because they distrusted a strong central government. This allowed states to act as they wished regarding important issues like slavery.

Pennsylvania was the first state to abolish slavery. It did so in 1780, three years before the war ended. However, it did not grant freedom to those who were currently slaves; it allowed for their children to be freed when they reached the age of twenty-eight.

A slave owner's dilemma

George Washington was the richest man in America in his day. Mount Vernon, his eight-thousand-acre plantation in Fairfax County, Virginia, resembled a small village, with its stables, smokehouse, bakery, icehouse, spinning house, and huts for nearly two hundred slaves. In 1775, when he became commander in chief of the Continental Army, Washington took one of his slaves, a young man named William Lee, with him to Massachusetts. Lee remained at Washington's side throughout the war as a servant. Washington liked Lee, allowing him to bring his wife, a free woman, to live at Mount Vernon after the war. This was not a common thing for slave owners to do.

While fighting for his own liberty, Washington had questioned the morality of slavery. In 1786, he told friends that he wished for a plan that would outlaw slavery. However, Washington was part of the South's economic system, and he never devised the plan. When he died in 1799, he provided that his slaves would be freed upon his wife's death. William Lee received immediate freedom and a small pension.

Massachusetts was the strongest antislavery state. Its constitution, introduced in 1780, was inspired by the Declaration of Independence when it stated that "all men are born free and equal." Consequently, a runaway slave named Quok Walker was able in 1781 to successfully sue his master for beating him after discovering his whereabouts. Walker's master was unsuccessful in suing the white man who had taken his slave in and given him a job. This important court case all but ended slavery in Massachusetts.

Black Presence Expands as War Continues

In 1776, colonists were still far from becoming a nation. Having declared independence from England, they now had to win it by force. This proved difficult as England's military was larger and better trained than the Continental Army. The British military force also included American Indians, American Loyalists, African-Americans, and German soldiers under the command of King George III. The Germans were called Hessians because they came from the German state of Hesse-Kassel. The Hessians were actually mercenary soldiers who were hired by the British to fight. Altogether, England had about fifty thousand soldiers in the New World at any one time.

The Continental Army never had more than fifteen thousand men, even after the length of service was extended to three years. Many American men were unaffected by the tax laws and other political issues and did not fight for either side. They preferred to serve in state militias, with their frequently inept elected officers. Militias required men only for short periods in nearby battles.

This is a tin sculpture of Hessian soldiers that is now part of an American folk art collection. During the American Revolution, Hessians (soldiers from the German state of Hesse-Kassel) were paid by the British to help them fight the war.

Conditions were harsh in the army, where food, clothing, and regular pay were all scarce. Disease spread through the camps, killing many. Some deserted in despair.

In 1777, the Continental Congress set quotas requiring each state to supply a certain number of men for the army. States had trouble filling the quotas and so recruited slaves, despite laws against slaves in the military. Some states changed their laws, with congressional support. The military draft — gathering names of eligible individuals and then calling them to service — was unknown.

Massachusetts passed the most liberal law concerning slaves and military service. In 1778, it ruled that any slave accepted into the military would be declared free. The state would pay his master an amount equal to his value on the slave market, and Congress would then pay the state. New York offered a land grant to any person who delivered his slave to the military — but did not offer freedom to the slave!

In the South, Maryland was the only state to allow slave enlistment. Virginia allowed only free people of color to serve, but white men brought their slaves to military headquarters anyway, claiming they were free.

Faceless, Unrewarded Soldiers

Blacks fought for America in all the major battles, but they seldom received recognition. They usually served as infantry privates, often assigned to unarmed positions, such as orderlies, servants, or cooks. Some were not listed by name on the rolls but as "A Negro Man" or "A Negro, name not known." Blacks usually fought side by side with whites but occasionally comprised their own unit, as did the First Regiment from Rhode Island, with 125 men, about one-third of them free.

Since Blacks could substitute for white men who had been drafted, there was not a regiment in the entire army that did not have some people of African descent. Blacks also served in the Continental Navy, which, like the army, was established in 1775. They often worked as pilots, steering small naval vessels through tricky inland waters they had learned to navigate as boys.

Edward Hector was among a few Black patriots assigned to the artillery. At the Battle of Brandywine in southeastern Pennsylvania in 1777, Hector refused to retreat. As patriots pulled back, he used guns found on the field to protect his horses and ammunition wagon. Hector's valor was not recognized until fifty years later, when the Pennsylvania legislature awarded him forty dollars. Jordan Freeman was another unsung African-American hero. He died at the Battle of Groton Heights in Connecticut in 1781. An orderly, Freeman helped kill a British officer in hand-to-hand combat after scaling the walls of a fort.

Thousands of Blacks also helped the American effort as civilians. Slaves were hired out to the military as carpenters, blacksmiths, and laborers. They felled trees or destroyed bridges to block the enemy, and they repaired roads. In 1776, just before New York City was taken by the British, all slave or free men were ordered to report with shovels to fortify the city. People of color also served as messengers, guides, and spies.

Foreign Forces Help the Americans

The colonists did not have enough money, supplies, or soldiers to win the war on their own. France, the Netherlands, and Spain gave cash gifts and loans to the Continental Congress. France also supplied weapons to help defeat England. In 1778, France also began supplying soldiers and warships. This was after the terrible winter of 1777-78, in which nearly one-fourth of George Washington's ten-thousand-man army was wiped out by disease, malnutrition, and the cold at the camp in Valley Forge, Pennsylvania, near Philadelphia. Spain entered the war in 1779, and the following year, the Netherlands began supplying troops.

Many Europeans arrived on their own, seeking adventure and a chance to help the American cause. Among them was Count Casimir Pulaski from Poland, a skilled cavalryman, killed at Savannah, Georgia, in 1778, a defeat for the Americans that led to British control over Georgia. Another Pole, Thaddeus Kosciusko, was a military engineer who helped rebuild Fort Ticonderoga, New York, near the Canadian border, after its capture from the British early in the war. Baron Friedrich von Steuben, a skilled drillmaster from Prussia, helped train the Continental Army at Valley Forge.

A Frenchman Against Slavery

Perhaps the most famous of the foreign recruits was the Marquis de Lafayette, a wealthy French aristocrat who was drawn to the notion of personal liberty. Lafayette arrived in 1777 at age nineteen and was commissioned a major general.

Lafayette was impressed with the privileges and quality of life that the average American colonist enjoyed. At first, he believed African slaves to be better off than the French peasants, which says something about how terrible conditions must have been in his own country. Eventually, however, Lafayette spoke out against slavery. After the war, he established a plantation on which slaves were educated and trained for freedom.

It is possible that an African slave named James helped Lafayette alter his views. In 1781, James served under Lafayette in Virginia as a spy, infiltrating Benedict Arnold's British camp to discover his battle plans. Lafayette so commended James's work that the Virginia assembly gave him his freedom. James took Lafayette's name, in tribute to his French hero. A number of years after the war, the Marquis de Lafayette visited America, visiting James Lafayette when he passed through Richmond.

More Fighting on the Frontier

Fighting continued on the frontier throughout the war, with Indian and British forces allied against the American colonists. The Cherokee in the Southeast lost much of their land as a result of the fighting. The same thing happened to the Iroquois, whose fighting centered on the area around Albany, New York, and extended as far as the Ohio Valley. Mohawk chief Joseph Brant and two Seneca chiefs, Cornplanter

The Marquis de Lafayette leads the calvary in battle. Lafayette became a lifelong opponent of slavery after his stay in America, and he helped establish an antislavery movement in Europe.

and Old Smoke, led the Native warriors who had remained loyal to the British. These included warriors of the Mohawk, Seneca, Cayuga, and Onondaga. Some battles pitted them against their former Oneida and Tuscarora allies who had sided with the colonists.

Brant's main concern was saving Iroquois land, not killing people, and usually he would give settlers and Indians in his path time to escape or join his side before he attacked their forts and villages and took their supplies. Some did join Brant on the Loyalist side. Others fled. In many battles, Brant did not shoot people unless they took up arms against his side first.

Defeat of the Iroquois

There were two incidents on the northeastern frontier that caused colonists to lash out against the Iroquois. The first took place in Pennsylvania's Wyoming Valley, where militiamen at a fort fired on approaching Seneca, Cayuga, and Tory Rangers before they realized they were outnumbered. More than two hundred militiamen were killed, and many settlers who fled the area later died of hunger or exhaustion. The event came to be known as the Wyoming Massacre.

The second incident, which took place near Albany, was called the Cherry Valley Massacre. Indians killed thirteen soldiers and nearly thirty women and children in revenge for the destruction of their own large and ancient settlement.

In 1779, in reaction to the two massacres, George Washington ordered an all-out attack on Iroquois land. This campaign destroyed about forty Indian villages along with crops and orchards. While Indian women and children fled to refugee camps in Canada, Iroquois warriors continued their raids on Americans until after the war. But their once-powerful confederation collapsed, and they would never again occupy their homelands freely.

War and Southern Slave Life

The war's first battles took place in the North, where early opposition to English rule was strongest. After 1778, England turned its attention to the rebellion in the South. Savannah, Georgia, was taken in 1779, then Charleston, South Carolina, in early 1780. Before embarking on his Carolinas campaign, British commanding general Sir Henry Clinton issued what has been called the Phillipsburg Proclamation. It warned that all Blacks he captured would be sold as slaves. However, it promised that any slaves who deserted their masters for British service would receive protection.

Lord Dunmore's Proclamation at the beginning of the war, which promised freedom to slaves who joined the British, had sent many slaves rushing to the British side, but General Clinton's words caused a virtual stampede. Even the British were surprised at the response. Thousands of men, women, and children fled farms and plantations alone, in pairs, or in groups of family and friends, despite the risks of detection.

They served the British military according to their skills and abilities, performing jobs that kept the war going. They built barracks and bridges, repaired boats and roads, and butchered meat for the troops. They worked in hospitals as orderlies and nurses. They even made cartridges for bullets. Those who were captured as slaves of rebel masters were also put to work, with the promise of freedom when the war ended.

Blacks served the British on the battlefield in the same ways they served the colonists, but there was one exception. Unlike the rebels, the British used

A dangerous journey to freedom

Old Ross, a fifty-six-year-old woman, became a quiet hero during the Revolutionary War when she helped a group of fellow slaves reach British lines after they fled Mary Thomas's South Carolina plantation. The group Old Ross led to safety included her grown daughters, Celia and Country Sue; her grown son, Dick; Celia's husband, Cato; and Elsey, Old Ross's granddaughter. Several nonfamily members were in the group, including Kate, a recent arrival from Angola.

Large groups of runaways increased the chances of being caught. The fact that this group and others took the risk shows their sense of kinship and determination to stay together. Slaves often were separated from friends and relatives by uncaring owners. Given the chance, however, they wanted to stay together. In 1779, the British offered all southern slaves freedom in exchange for labor and loyalty.

Blacks extensively in the cavalry. When he saw how good the British cavalry was, the Marquis de Lafayette urged George Washington to put African-Americans on horseback.

At the height of the war in the rural South, life was chaotic. Men were off fighting, crops were destroyed by armies, and animals were stolen. In many cases, slaves who stayed stopped functioning as slaves, simply doing what was needed to survive. In a letter to a family member, Thomas Pinckney told how the British had raided his Carolina plantation, taking nineteen slaves. He complained that the sick women, young children, and five men who remained acted "perfectly free" by paying no attention to their overseer.

Life was not easy for slaves who remained at home. There were shortages of food and clothing in winter months. Many slaves did not flee because of the dangers of the journey. If they were caught by the colonial forces, death was almost certain.

The Phillipsburg Proclamation, like Lord Dunmore's Proclamation before it, was designed to bolster the British military and deprive colonists of labor. The slaves who responded did so not for political reasons but as a vote against slavery. As many as ten thousand slaves in South Carolina and Georgia joined the British. Others escaped into forest or swamp to survive as well as they could.

Dangers to Women and Children

Life was difficult for colonial women and children left at home. Men who knocked on the doors of their isolated country homes asking for food and shelter might be fierce robbers disguised as soldiers. A bandit named Joseph Mulliner terrorized the New Jersey countryside until he was caught and hanged. Sometimes soldiers turned villainous, as did the band of British cavalrymen who robbed and abused Eliza Wilkinson, a young widow, and her two sisters on their South Carolina plantation. The women fled to Charleston, as did many women and children in the state. Wilkinson later described the war as a time of "cruelty, bloodshed, and oppression, where neither age nor sex escaped the horrors of injustice and violence."

Hardships for the Poor

When cities were threatened by the war, residents fled to the country. Sarah Wister of Philadelphia was fifteen when the war began. Soon after fire devastated New York City in 1776, her family left Philadelphia for fear of a similar disaster there. They were among the lucky ones; living conditions deteriorated in Philadelphia and other cities. Fueled by a combination of poor sanitation, bad water, food shortages, and crowding, disease spread rapidly.

The poor, many of them Black, suffered most, as they could not afford medical treatment. Wister's best friend, Debby Norris, wrote to her that "Philadelphia is not as it used to be. You can scarce walk a square without seeing the shocking sight of a cart with five or six coffins in it. . . . Large pits are dug in the negroes' burying ground, and forty or fifty coffins are put in the same hole. This is really true. I do not exaggerate."

Working People Find a Voice

In order to survive the war years, many poor people organized against wealthy merchants who were charging high prices for food, firewood, and other necessities. Some of the offending merchants were Loyalists. Others were leading patriots, such as Robert Morris of Philadelphia, one of the signers of the Declaration of Independence. Morris was accused of driving up prices by keeping food off the market.

Tradesmen and unskilled laborers alike held town meetings, posted notices in the streets, and appealed to state and federal lawmakers for price controls and higher wages. They tried stronger tactics when these methods failed. In 1778, 150 sailors in Philadelphia struck for higher wages. Continental troops were called out to break the strike.

Angry poor people in Albany, New York, forced price gougers to stand on a platform in the marketplace until they promised to charge less. In Boston, one hundred women raided the warehouse of a merchant who wanted to drive prices up by hoarding coffee. In 1779, several people were killed in a riot in

Robert Morris was a leading patriot and signer of the Declaration of Independence. During the war, he was one of several businessmen, Tory and patriot alike, accused of driving up food prices, making an already difficult life even harder for the poor.

Deborah Sampson, female soldier

Deborah Sampson spent most of her Massachusetts childhood as an indentured servant, performing activities that most people considered boy's work. She plowed fields, cut and stacked hay, milked cows, and was a skilled carpenter. She also enjoyed learning, another activity that many people considered strictly for boys. Craving adventure when the war broke out, she ignored convention.

In 1782, when new recruits were desperately needed, she enlisted in the Continental Army, disguised as a man. She was wounded once and refused to go to the hospital for fear her identity would be discovered. According to her own account, she once removed a bullet from her thigh. Later, however, she was hospitalized with a dangerously high fever and her identity was discovered. Sampson was honorably discharged from the army. She worked as a farmhand, still preferring men's clothes. She eventually married a farmer and had three children. Years later, she petitioned the Massachusetts legislature for back pay the army had withheld. She received thirty-four pounds and a citation for her "extraordinary instance of female heroism."

Philadelphia that broke out after months of protests by local militiamen over skyrocketing food prices.

Even those who fled the cities were touched by the war. The Wister family of Philadelphia moved in with another family in a remote farmhouse near Valley Forge. As it turned out, the war moved into that area, too. Troops on either side camped within miles of the home, which soon became quarters for several American officers. The Wisters could hear firing from nearby battles, and they lived in fear that fighting would engulf their house.

A Young, War-Ravaged Nation

The war that began in April 1775 at Lexington and Concord, Massachusetts, dragged on for eight years. Fighting was never constant in any one area. Soldiers clashed in specific battles, then advanced or retreated to rest and train for the next attack. Warfare took place throughout the colonies and along the western frontier. Early in the war, there were battles in Canada as Americans tried unsuccessfully to capture Quebec and persuade white Canadians to join their side.

After 1778, many critical events took place at sea. Ships that sailed out of British ports were terrorized by American privateers — privately owned and manned ships that the American government authorized to attack enemy vessels. The patriots picked off cargo ships; by the end of the war, they had seized an estimated fifteen hundred vessels. This frequently cut off supplies headed to the New World for British troops. The English navy greatly outnumbered the colonists' ships but feared straying too far from England because the French were massing for an invasion of Great Britain that was planned but did not take place.

By 1780, the British held New York City and Philadelphia in the North and Charleston and Savannah in the South, along with most of Georgia. That same year, colonists stopped the British from taking control of the Carolinas, but the British burned and destroyed farms and plantations as they retreated, leaving the region in ruins. In 1781, the fighting centered on Virginia, where the colonists won a major battle in October at Yorktown and laid siege to the city. Yorktown proved to be the turning point of the war.

Two seafaring vessels fire at each other in a dramatic battle. What would become the U.S. Navy got its start during the Revolution and had an important impact on the outcome of the Revolution. By the end of the war, patriots had seized about fifteen hundred British vessels.

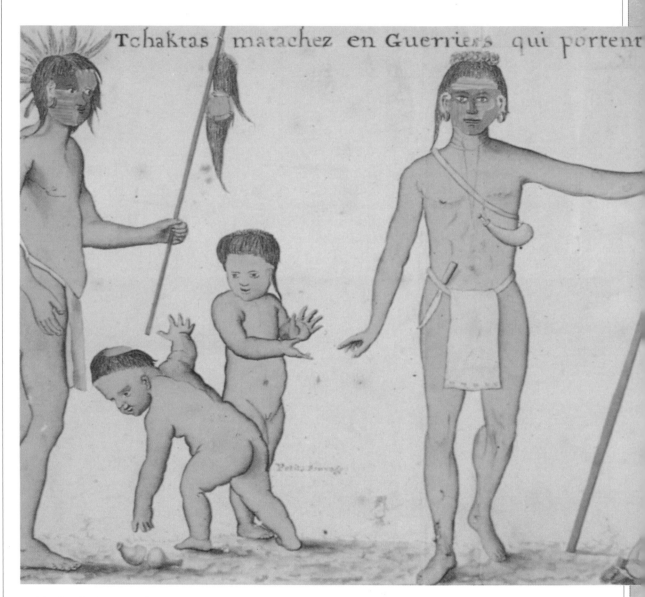

This sketch of seven Choctaw Indians by a European artist presents a romantic view of people that Europeans often mistakenly described as savages. The Choctaw and other Southeast tribes made great efforts to adapt to European customs and expectations, often through separate treaties with the government.

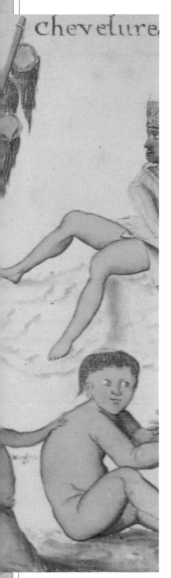

chevelure

Freedom Rings, But Not for All

In the summer and fall of 1781, several thousand slave men, women, and children followed British General Charles Cornwallis through Virginia to the little tobacco port of Yorktown. Their already difficult lives had been turned upside down by fighting that had burned homes and crops and sent many of their owners fleeing for safety. Everyone was suffering from food and clothing shortages, but slaves suffered most because they had so little. Many were starving and half-naked when the British came through, promising freedom.

Cornwallis's troops plundered as they marched. They ate food in their path like a swarm of locusts. Slaves went through closets in deserted plantation houses, helping themselves to fine clothes. They may have been turning the tables on their owners, but more likely they were trying to stay warm. They divided the finery so that one man could be seen wearing nothing but silk breeches and another an elegant shirt, while the woman beside him sported a lounging robe with a long train or a silk corset. Others fancied hats and wigs.

The parade ended sadly, however, with a long siege at Yorktown in October. The British and their Black followers were surrounded by a large force of American and French soldiers. The Africans serving the British worked to fortify Yorktown from attack. Throughout the long march, they had been nurses, maids, cooks, and orderlies, scrounging food for the big army. But as supplies and hopes dwindled, the British sent many Blacks away, back to slavery and punishment by their masters. Many died of illness in Yorktown.

The British surrendered on October 19, 1781, after nearly three weeks of siege. A new government rose to power in England five months later, and with much of the South now in ruins, the English had little interest in continuing the war. They needed to save the rest of their empire from the French and the Spanish. In April, peace talks between England and American representatives began in Paris.

British General Charles Cornwallis surrenders to American forces after the Battle of Yorktown in October 1781. This battle virtually ended the war, which would continue sporadically for two more years, but with no major battles, as the British began turning their attention to their empire in other parts of the world. Britain formally recognized the United States as an independent nation in 1783.

The fighting continued sporadically back home, but there were no more major battles. The war officially ended on September 3, 1783, when the peace treaty was signed.

In addition to sheer perseverance on the part of the American forces, other factors helped the ragtag revolutionaries overcome incredible odds to defeat the mighty British. For example, although the colonies were of great importance to the English, they had other holdings, such as India, that were much more profitable. In addition, the French, Spanish, and Dutch had joined the American side against their rival, England. Their combined might, particularly the sea power of the French and Spanish, was impressive. It helped the British realize that if they kept up their fight in America, they could well run the risk of keeping the colonies but losing their home island. And because they retained what is today eastern Canada, the British did not feel utterly defeated.

Diverse People with a Common Dream

After the war, America remained a land of numerous ethnic and religious backgrounds, many slaves, indentured servants, women, American Indians, free Blacks, and men with neither property nor the right to vote. It was still a land of many contradictions — a place where a poor man could obtain riches, as well as one where only a small number of people held great wealth. But it was also a land that had fought a war based on notions of equality and liberty for all.

Although many people did not yet have equal rights and freedom, there were few people at war's end who were unaware of the country's principles. It was this knowledge more than anything else that eventually helped unite Americans into one nation. It was also this knowledge that helped empower each oppressed group eventually to speak out for its rights.

New Paths to Black Freedom

Though the British betrayed Blacks who followed them to Yorktown, they did keep their promise to thousands who had joined their ranks during the war. It is estimated that at least fourteen thousand African-American men, women, and children left with the British soldiers who returned to England.

They sailed from Savannah, Charleston, and New York City to new lives in Florida, Canada, the West Indies, Europe, and Africa. Not all found the life of their dreams. Some were forced back into slavery or into poverty. But many did well, starting free communities in the Bahamas, for instance, and in Sierra Leone on the West Coast of Africa.

It is estimated that between eighty and one hundred thousand slaves left their owners during the war. (Thomas Jefferson believed Virginia alone lost thirty thousand slaves in 1781.) Many died of smallpox or fever in British military camps. Some were taken as slaves to Canada with their Loyalist owners. Some escaped to freedom in the cities. Others settled in the swamplands of Virginia, North Carolina, Georgia, and South Carolina, where they built cabins and farmed.

Those promised freedom for fighting on the American side did, in most cases, receive it. Those whose owners did not keep their word were able to appeal to the authorities. Ned Griffin was freed by the North Carolina legislature after his owner reenslaved him, and Jack Arabas brought successful court action against his master in Connecticut for the same reason.

A slave receives her freedom from her white owners. Many African-Americans acquired freedom as a result of changing attitudes after the war. During this time, Black leaders arose to speak out for their people's rights. In this engraving, the white owners are portrayed as lofty and a bit indifferent to the slave, who is shown in a position of gratitude and subservience.

The American Revolution taught Blacks that they could make demands on white society. Even before war's end, they began to speak for their rights. In 1780, seven free people of color petitioned the Massachusetts legislature for the right to vote, pointing out that they were subject to taxation without representation by the new American government. In Boston, a group of Blacks asked for school funding, something whites already had. In Norfolk, Virginia, they asked for the right to testify in court.

Black Clergy Speak Out. Many African-American clergy were outspoken, despite threats to their lives. David George, George Liele, and Andrew Bryan pioneered the African Baptist Church while still slaves. George and Liele left America with the British. Liele later established the Baptist Church in Jamaica, and George continued his work in Nova Scotia, Canada, then Sierra Leone. Bryan bought his freedom when his master died, and with help from white Baptists, raised money to build the First African Baptist Church of Savannah.

Lemuel Haynes was a minuteman at Lexington and Concord and became the first African-American minister of the Congregational Church in America. Absalom Jones, an early leader of the African Methodist Church in Philadelphia, helped organize a school for African-American children, created and directed an insurance company, and organized protests against Black civil-rights violations.

Raising White Consciousness. The revolutionary fight for equality reached white people who had never before questioned slavery. Many owners, especially in the North, freed their slaves or made arrangements for freedom when they died. Large aboliltionist societies formed in northern states and in Maryland. Members worked to protect free African-Americans from being sold back into slavery and provided them with education and job training. One by one,

Speaking out for African-American dignity

"I suppose it is a truth too well attested to you, to need a proof here, that we are a race of beings, who have long labored under the abuse and censure of the world; that we have long been looked upon with an eye of contempt; and that we have long been considered rather as brutish than human, and scarcely capable of mental endowments. . . . I apprehend you will embrace every opportunity to eradicate that train of absurd and false ideas and opinions, which so generally prevails with respect to us; and that your sentiments are concurrent with mine, which are, that one universal Father hath given being to us all; and that he hath not only made us all of one flesh, but that he hath also, without partiality, afforded us all the same sensations and endowed us all with the same facilities."

— From a letter written in 1791 to Thomas Jefferson, then secretary of state, by Benjamin Banneker of Maryland. Banneker was born a free person of color in 1731. He was a self-taught mathematician, astronomer, and surveyor who helped design the nation's new capital, Washington, D.C. The above letter was written after Jefferson claimed Blacks were less intelligent than whites.

northern states followed the example of Pennsylvania and Massachusetts, passing laws that provided for the gradual emancipation of all slaves.

Slavery existed in the North until well into the 1800s, but by 1804, all northern states had laws abolishing it. Southern leaders also spoke out against slavery, but there was not enough support to pass antislavery laws. Virginia, however, made it easier for owners to free their slaves, doing away with a law that required them to first obtain consent from the legislature. Virginia also decreed the death penalty to anyone who knowingly sold a free person as a slave.

The number of free African-Americans increased after the war in Virginia, Maryland, and North Carolina, and these states gradually limited or banned the slave trade. Nevertheless, the slave population grew in the South as African-Americans continued to be born into slavery. South Carolina and Georgia were more tied to slavery than ever with the advent of cotton as an important crop. These states stepped up the slave trade after the war.

White Prejudice Grows. Many owners enforced even stricter slave codes after the war to prevent revolts. Southern states passed laws that reflected the growing racial prejudices of white slave owners. These prejudices arose from feelings of white superiority. But they also arose from the fear of violence at the hands of slaves who suffered from miserable treatment and resented a system that excluded them from the calls for freedom that were rising up around them. So in many ways, white prejudice fed on itself, resulting in a legal system that looked the other way, for instance, when an owner killed a slave. Yet the same system demanded death for a slave who killed a cruel overseer.

Eventually, in response to continued unrest, some southern states, such as Virginia and North Carolina, passed laws giving African-Americans some legal protection, such as the right to trial by jury and the right to be represented by a lawyer. However, when cases came to court in the South, most judges and juries automatically ruled in favor of owners. The double legal standard against African-Americans would continue well into the twentieth century.

Rights for Slaves. During the war, some owners realized that they could no longer control their slaves' lives; these slaves enjoyed some independence. After the war, some owners allowed slaves to sell produce grown in their own small gardens. Slaves also could sell baskets, chairs, wooden bowls, and other items made on their own time. They could hire themselves out to other plantations for field work on Sundays. Others worked freely as butchers, tailors, carpenters, masons, and cobblers. They were required to give a percentage of their earnings to their owners, but they saved the rest for their freedom.

Big Losses for American Indians

The British did not make provisions for their Native allies in the peace treaty they signed with the colonists. According to the 1783 treaty, England recognized the former colonies as the United States, an independent nation, granting the former colonists all land from the Atlantic Ocean to the Mississippi River and from Canada to Florida. England gave Florida to Spain. The treaty ignored the fact that the territory handed to the United States was Indian land.

Catherine Rolleston's Mohawk legacy

Catherine Rolleston was the daughter of Dutch-American settlers in Pennsylvania. In 1774, when she was thirteen, Mohawks attacked her village in revenge for the massacre of relatives of Seneca Chief Logan. They found Catherine alone in her house, the rest of her family apparently having fled without her. The Mohawk took Catherine with them. She was adopted into the family of Teyonhahwekea, one of the most important chiefs in the Iroquois Confederacy. Catherine learned the Mohawk language and customs.

During the Revolutionary War, these Mohawk moved to safety in Niagara, Canada. It was the responsibility of Chief Teyonhahwekea and his family to transport the tribe's most important treasures. According to family legend, Catherine wrapped the peace pipe, silver jewelry, and other treasures in old cloth, so that it looked like she was carrying a bundle of rags on her back. In this way, the soldiers who accompanied them on their journey did not know the nature of her burden and did not steal it.

Catherine later settled with her people on land the British gave them along the Grand River in Ontario, Canada. She married George Martin, an important Mohawk chieftain. Among her many descendants was her great-granddaughter, E. Pauline Johnson, who in the early twentieth century became one of Canada's most celebrated poets.

Indians were forced to negotiate separate treaties with the Americans, most of whom regarded them as defeated enemies. U.S. officials held meetings with Indian representatives, informing them that their lands had been surrendered by the British and that they must now recognize U.S. control. Indians were shocked and angered. They had lost people, crops, even entire villages in the war. And they had been good allies to the British.

Creek and Choctaw in the South had succeeded until the war's end in keeping Savannah in British hands. The Iroquois continued their raids on Americans long after the British surrendered at Yorktown. They had not admitted defeat and could not understand how the British could leave them to deal with land-hungry settlers. Because white settlement of Indian lands had ceased during the war, Native people had good reason to prolong the fight. When the conflict ended, settlers and land speculators once again moved west.

Creating Reservations. After the war, the U.S. government set aside land for Indians within portions of their former territories. Shawnee, Delaware, Wyandot, some Ottawa, and Ojibwa were given reservations in Ohio. The Iroquois League, including the Tuscarora and Oneida, who had supported the Americans in the war, received small reservations in New York. Many Mohawk and other Iroquois followers of Joseph Brant went to Canada, where the British honored the Indians' loyalty with land along the Grand River in what is now Ontario. Their town became known as Brantford, and Joseph Brant remained an important leader.

Taking Indian Land. Indians in the Great Lakes region soon found their new treaties violated by white settlers. Individual states had more power than the federal government, so agreements between Congress and Native people often were undermined by the states, whose citizens had no sympathy for Indians. Their prejudices had been fueled by the war's fierce fighting. Also, many of these people could not afford land in parts of the United States already settled. They did not know Indian culture and did not understand the spiritual connection between Indians and the land. They wanted to fulfill their own dreams.

The prevailing mood of white Americans was reflected in these words by an army officer: "The people of Kentucky will carry on private expeditions against the Indians and kill them whenever they meet them, and I do not believe that there is a jury in all Kentucky who would punish a man for it."

The U.S. Congress attempted to protect what rights the Indians still retained. Congress warned settlers in 1783 not to purchase or settle Indian lands. In 1785, Congress told settlers to stay south of the Ohio River. The federal government sent troops to evict squatters who ignored these orders, but their efforts failed. White settlers kept coming, and Congress did not send enough troops to enforce the law.

There was much fighting between Indians and white settlers in the Great Lakes region. In 1787, the Northwest Ordinance, enacted by the U.S. Congress, encouraged European-Americans to settle the present states of Ohio, Indiana, Illinois, and Wisconsin. Battles grew more heated and involved many tribes, including the Miami, Potawatomi, Menominee, Illinois, Sauk, Fox, Winnebago, and Shawnee. Fighting continued into the nineteenth century, with Indian lands whittled into ever smaller pieces.

Troubled Times in the Southeast. The situation was difficult and confusing for southeastern tribes after the war. Their lands lay in areas claimed by several governments, so they could not be sure whom they could trust in negotiating treaties. The Cherokee, for instance, occupied land claimed by North Carolina, South Carolina, and Georgia, and in the far South by France and Spain. The new central government of the United States also claimed much of this land. Some claims overlapped areas belonging to the Creek and the

These Cherokee Indians of the early 1800s wear clothes that strongly reflect European styles of the time. Despite their efforts to adapt to European ways and deal with the U.S. government through separate treaties, they and members of other Southeast tribes lost their lands and were eventually removed by force to Oklahoma.

Chickasaw. Worse, government agents who negotiated treaties often acted for land speculators. They went after the most land for the lowest possible price.

The Cherokee, Creek, Choctaw, and Chickasaw reluctantly made separate treaties with the U.S. government. Each tribe gave up much land in return for promises that new land would be protected. As in the North, white settlers moved onto Indian lands anyway, with bloodshed for years to come.

Adopting European Ways. In the troubled years following the American Revolution, southeastern Indians abandoned ancient traditions. Some of these changes came through intermarriage with the whites. Colonial men who had fought for the British married Native women. They often moved their families from tribal towns to farms where they lived independently. They had many children but did not teach them their Native language and religion and did not allow the wife's brother to teach them, as was the custom in matrilineal tribes.

Other southeastern Indians began adopting more and more white customs in the hopes that this would make them acceptable to their European-American neighbors. Their farms resembled white farms, with livestock, cotton, and wheat. They learned European techniques for such trades as spinning, weaving, and blacksmithing and started their own businesses. They purchased slaves, wore European clothing, and sent their sons to missionary schools.

Adopting white ways helped southeastern tribes become less dependent on trade with the European-Americans, but it turned them away from their own chiefs and religious leaders. European-Americans failed to accept the Natives as equals, even though they were granted many of the liberties and rights under the law that the colonists had sought in the Declaration of Independence.

American Women Speak Out for Rights

As we have learned, colonial women played an important role in the Revolution. They performed jobs that kept the new nation alive while its men were at war. They farmed and worked in many trades and professions. They followed their men to the battlefields and tended to their needs, sometimes even taking up arms. They also participated in public affairs, boycotting British goods, campaigning against the British tea tax, and confronting merchants who gouged them with high prices.

This was considerable progress for European-American women, who had previously lived in the shadows of their husbands, brothers, and fathers. They had no voting rights, and if they were married, could not own property. Many had no formal education and could not read or write.

As a result of their enlarged role, women began to speak up for greater rights under the law even before the war ended. In 1776, Abigail Adams urged her husband, John Adams, to "remember the ladies" in the new code of laws that he and other members of the Continental Congress would devise. She asked him not to give men as much power over women as they had held in the past. "Remember all men would be tyrants if they could," she said in a letter written while he was meeting with the Continental Congress. If men did not give women their due rights, she warned, women would rebel.

Others spoke out for women's rights after the war. Mary Wollstonecraft of England wrote a book about women's rights that was read widely in the United States. In it, she urged women to be more assertive. She warned that men often confused soft-spokenness with weakness.

Women did not get the vote after the Revolutionary War except in New Jersey, and that right was revoked in 1807. After the war, there was a tendency by men to push women back into dependent roles at home as wives and mothers. Nonetheless, American society was changing, and women were making strides. The daughters and granddaughters of revolutionary-era women would in greater and greater numbers go to school, hold jobs, campaign against slavery, work to improve conditions in prisons and poorhouses, and consistently speak out for more rights for themselves. The roles of women in the Revolution were omitted from many history books written by European-American men.

Women line up to vote for the first time in New Jersey, the only state that granted voting rights to women following the Revolution. They lost this right in 1807. Although women throughout the country asked for more rights after the war, many men feared they were becoming too independent.

Poverty Remains, but Doors Open

Poverty did not go away after the American Revolution, but in some important ways, the war improved the lot of people in the lower economic classes. Many poor, for instance, received land in exchange for fighting for the revolutionary cause. (Unfortunately, this land was often on the frontier and conflicted with the rights of American Indians to retain their homelands.) Indentured servants

This map shows the way the eastern part of North America looked in the decades following the Revolution. The map shows the early United States, areas controlled by the French (Louisiana) and Spanish (Florida), and British and French sections of Canada. Immediately following the war, a great population shift occurred as thousands of people who had supported England left the United States for Canada.

also received freedom as a result of enlisting in the army. In New York, people spoke out against the indentured servant system because it robbed people of their liberties. The system remained in existence, however, for many years.

The colonial tradespeople and laborers who had supported the revolutionary cause in the northern cities did not receive much power in the new American government. However, like many African-Americans, they learned that they could speak out against injustices and that their words and actions could make a difference. These feelings carried over into the workplace.

Where once they had regarded their employer as a benefactor or guardian whose deeds they could not question, they now knew employers sometimes took advantage of them, demanding long hours in unsafe surroundings for low pay. They learned to band together with workers in their city and in other cities to demand better conditions. The revolutionary fight for "life, liberty, and the pursuit of happiness" thus planted the seeds for what became known as the American labor movement.

The Changing Map

There was a great shifting of populations in North America as a result of the Revolutionary War. As many as eighty thousand people in all departed. Some returned to England or settled in Louisiana. Most made their way to Canada, still English territory but only sparsely populated by European settlers. They settled in what are now Ontario, Quebec, New Brunswick, and Nova Scotia. Loyalists included American Indians, African-Americans, and colonists of English, Scottish, Irish, French, and German ancestry. They helped make Canada the multicultural society it is today.

Many people moved onto unsettled frontier, and others flocked to new cities, abandoning coastal cities that had been badly damaged by war. State governments moved with them. Richmond became the capital of Virginia instead of Williamsburg. Albany replaced New York City as the capital of New York. Columbia became the capital of South Carolina instead of Charleston, and Augusta became the capital of Georgia instead of Savannah. The new state capitals were more convenient to the frontiers and were accessible to trade of tobacco, cotton, and other crops.

Some people also felt safer in the new, less crowded cities. During the Revolution, rural people had come to distrust the larger cities, with their many problems and ties to British wealth. A general suspicion of large cities exists today among people in less populated regions of the country.

Other patterns emerged after the Revolutionary War. The northeastern seaboard cities, which had been centers of political activity against the king, have remained, to a great extent, politically liberal, whereas southern regions have remained politically conservative. In the 1800s, leaders who stood for the rights of the oppressed continued to arise in Boston, Philadelphia, and New York. In 1835, workers in Philadelphia successfully struck for a ten-hour workday. Dorothea Dix helped improve terrible conditions in Boston prisons and poorhouses in the 1840s.

Dorothea Dix fought for the rights of oppressed people in Boston during the 1800s. She was part of a movement, born in the years following the American Revolution, that worked to improve conditions for workers, prisoners, and the homeless.

The Revolution's Legacy

The American Revolution caused waves of excitement around the world. Despite imperfections and inconsistencies, it offered hope to oppressed people everywhere. In 1789, revolution broke out in France as impoverished peasants

and working people vented their anger at the unlimited power and extrava-
gance of wealthy royal leaders. The French had their own writers and political
leaders to lead them, but the recent success of the Americans offered inspira-
tion, too. France did not become a democracy as a result of this war, but the king
lost absolute power and the common person gained some rights. The middle
class also gained power.

In the 1800s, revolutions hit other countries in Europe, including Belgium,
the Netherlands, and Denmark. These wars reduced the power of the monarch
and introduced basic liberties for the average person. As white people became
more conscious of their own rights, they continued to question slavery. Throughout the 1800s, European countries outlawed slavery. The United States banned
it in 1865, though not without a civil war.

A Democracy Is Born

In 1787, several years after the Revolution ended, American leaders again gathered in Philadephia to write the Constitution of the United States. The Articles of Confederation created during the war held the thirteen states together
too loosely to work as a national government. The Constitution that replaced
the Articles is similar to the democratic plan that held the Iroquois League
together for many years. The framers of the Constitution probably borrowed
from several plans as their model, including earlier colonial forms of government.
They undoubtedly even looked to Britain, even though that nation had a
monarchy. But Britain's was a constitutional monarchy — a monarchy that
had unwritten constitutional guarantees that must have appealed to early U.S.
lawmakers. The early framers of the U.S. Constitution also copied from Britain
the idea of having two legislative houses (the U.S. Senate and the House of
Representatives, which together make up the U.S. Congress). Despite the fact
that Americans had rebelled against the British, there was much about the
British system that was familiar to them, so they borrowed and modified what
they felt had worked for them as colonists.

After being ratified, or approved, by nine of the thirteen states, the Constitution went into effect on June 21, 1788. The remaining four states ratified
it by 1790. In 1789, Congress added ten amendments to the Constitution, and

First Amendment protects basic freedoms

"Congress shall make no law respecting an establishment of religion or pro-
hibiting the free exercise thereof; or abridging the freedom of speech or of the
press; or the right of the people peaceably to assemble, and to petition the
government for a redress of grievances."

— The first of ten amendments to the U.S. Constitution, known as the Bill
of Rights and ratified on December 13, 1791. The First Amendment has served
to this day to protect the basic freedoms of U.S. citizens. The leaders of some
states refused to accept the Constitution unless it also included a bill of rights.

these became law in 1791. Known as the Bill of Rights, these amendments lay out and protect individual liberties. The First Amendment of the Bill of Rights is often called upon today to protect such basic rights as free speech, freedom of the press, and freedom of religion.

The democratic principles of the American Revolution live on today around the world in struggles against oppression. As Phillis Wheatley, the former African slave, wrote more than two hundred years ago, "In every human breast, God has Implanted a Principle, that we call love of freedom." In modern times, the people of Nicaragua, Guatemala, El Salvador, Argentina, Angola, South Africa, China, Cambodia, Vietnam, Bosnia, Palestine, and Haiti have died and continue to die for individual freedoms as basic as the right to have food and clean water to drink.

In our own country, the struggle for "life, liberty, and the pursuit of happiness" continues as well. We live in a multicultural society with many diverse interest groups. All of these groups — women, African-Americans, Indian people, people with disabilities, poor people, gays and lesbians, senior citizens, right-wing conservatives, to name just a few — know they can exercise their constitutional right to speak out when their freedoms are threatened.

Today, despite persistent divisions between people of different racial, ethnic, and economic groups — and particularly the ever-widening gap between the wealthy and the poor — the United States remains a country where the common man, woman, and child can speak for individual freedoms. Everyone has the right to disagree and the right to try to change systems that no longer work fairly. That is the rich legacy of the American Revolution.

American leaders gather in Philadelphia in 1787 to write the U.S. Constitution. This important document forms the framework of a democratic government and, with its Bill of Rights, protects basic freedoms for all U.S. citizens.

CHRONOLOGY

1763 England wins the Seven Years' War (also known as the French and Indian War) and becomes a major power in colonial North America; Potawatomie, Huron, and Ottawa tribes fight the British in a war known as Pontiac's Uprising; King George III issues the Proclamation of 1763, which seeks to prevent colonial expansion west of the Appalachian Mountains

1764 England begins passing laws that put restraints on the colonial American economy

1765 England passes the Quartering Act of 1765, requiring colonists to help support British troops in colonial America; England passes the Stamp Act amidst complaints of "taxation without representation"; the Sons of Liberty are organized to protest new British laws

1766 Widespread protests and rioting in the colonies lead England to repeal the Stamp Act

1767 The Townshend Acts place duties on imported British goods, including tea

1770 British soldiers fire on civilians at the Boston Massacre, killing five

1773 The Tea Act is passed, and angry colonists dump shiploads of tea into the sea at the Boston Tea Party; the abolitionist movement gathers momentum in the North

1774 England passes the Intolerable Acts, closing Boston Harbor and restricting the activities of the Massachusetts legislature; representatives of the colonies meet in Philadelphia at the first Continental Congress; slaves in Massachusetts petition the legislature for freedom; Lord Dunmore's War between the Shawnee and British is fought over white settlement of Shawnee lands

1775 The American Revolution begins at Lexington and Concord, Massachusetts; Second Continental Congress convenes and appoints George Washington as commander in chief of the new Continental Army; Lord Dunmore's Proclamation offers freedom to slaves who join the British side

1776 The Continental Congress adopts the Declaration of Independence and the colonies declare themselves states; the British capture New York City

1777 France joins the fight against England after the colonists win an important battle at Saratoga, New York; the Continental Army spends a cold, hungry winter at Valley Forge, Pennsylvania; war spreads to the western frontier as Indians and Loyalists battle patriots

1778 England focuses its war campaign in the South, capturing Savannah, Georgia

1779 Spain enters the war on the American side

1780 The Netherlands enters the war as an American ally; Charleston, South Carolina, surrenders to the British; American General Benedict Arnold joins the British side; Americans win an important victory at Kings Mountain, Georgia; Pennsylvania is the first state to abolish slavery

1781 American and French forces defeat the British at Yorktown, Virginia, in the last major battle of the war; the states approve the Articles of Confederation, which unite them under a central government

1782 Peace negotiations begin in Paris

1783 Treaty of Paris is signed on September 3, recognizing the former colonies as an independent nation called the United States; Massachusetts Supreme Court outlaws slavery

1787 Congress signs the U.S. Constitution into law at Philadelphia on September 17

1789 George Washington is named first president of the United States; the first U.S. Congress under the Constitution meets in New York City

1791 Ten amendments known as the Bill of Rights are added to the U.S. Constitution

GLOSSARY

abolitionism an organized movement against the practice of slavery

acculturation the process by which one group of people acquires the customs and traits of another group, often through prolonged contact

boycott an organized effort to avoid business dealings with a person, business, or group, usually for the purpose of making a statement or complaint about that group or attempting to force that group to change a policy or practice

consciousness (in politics or social behavior) personal awareness or concern, usually for a social or political cause

conservative in politics, a way of thinking that favors existing conditions and institutions

confederation a league of persons, tribes, states, or nations joined together for a common purpose

draft conscription; a method of selecting people for military service without their consent

emancipation the act of freeing people from slavery or any other form of restraint or control

empire a political realm with extensive territory and power

hypocrisy the act of claiming a belief or a feeling that one does not possess; saying one thing and behaving in an opposing way

ideal an ultimate, not always obtainable goal that upholds a standard of perfection or excellence

insurrection an act of rebelling against an established authority or government

iniquitous vicious, wicked, or extremely unjust

legacy a gift that is received from events in the past or from an ancestor

liberal in politics, one who is open to thinking and actions that may be different from the traditional or established ways

manumission the process of formally freeing someone from slavery

matriarchal pertaining to a family, group, or political system that is dominated or heavily influenced by women

militia a group of citizens who by law can be called up in an emergency for military service

negotiate to talk to others in such a way as to reach a settlement on a disputed matter

quota	a designated number or amount considered to be a desired or proportionate amount; in modern usage, quotas have become associated with fixed numbers of people from certain racial, ethnic, or gender groups hired for jobs or admitted into schools
persecute	to harass in a way intended to injure
principle	a fundamental law or belief
proclamation	something that is solemnly and officially declared
radical	characterized by considerable, often extreme, departure from the usual or traditional
reservation	(as pertaining to American Indians) a section of land set aside by a government for use by a designated group that is generally smaller than the amount of land that group previously claimed
refugee	someone who flees a region, country, or political power to escape danger or persecution
speculator	someone who buys or sells something (often land or property) with the sole purpose of profiting from ups and downs in the market
tariff	a sum of money that a government requires be paid on goods being imported into, or in some cases exported from, a country
treaty	a formal, written contract of agreement between two or more political powers

FURTHER READING

Deloria, Vine, Jr. *God Is Red: A Native View of Religion*. Golden, Co.: North American Press, 1992.

Ehle, John. *Trail of Tears: The Rise and Fall of the Cherokee Nation*. New York: Anchor Books, 1988.

Frey, Sylvia R. *Water From the Rock: Black Resistance in a Revolutionary Age*. Princeton, N.J.: Princeton University Press, 1991.

Green, Rayna. *Women in American Indian Society*. New York: Chelsea House Publishers, 1992.

Kaplan, Sidney and Emma Nogrady Kaplan. *The Black Presence in the Era of the American Revolution*. Amherst: University of Massachusetts Press, 1989.

Magee, Joan. *Loyalist Mosaic: A Multi-Ethnic Heritage*. Toronto: Dundurn Press, 1984.

Nash, Gary B. *Race and Revolution*. Madison, Wis.: Madison House, 1990.

Weatherford, Jack. *Native Roots: How the Indians Enriched America*. New York: Crown Publishers, 1991.

White, Deborah Gray. *Arn't I A Woman?: Female Slaves in the Plantation South*. New York: W.W. Norton, 1985.

Zinn, Howard. *A People's History of the United States*, second ed. New York: Harper Perennial, 1990.